Don't Think What You Want:

FREEDOM OF THOUGHT WITHOUT THIS BOOK

By: JACK CONNOR

Contents

Annotation

Dear reader,

how am I supposed to address you? Should I always use the masculine and feminine form of address? I tried exactly that for a few pages and discarded it after a short time. I just didn't find this approach elegant. For this reason I decided to only choose the male form. I do this knowing that I am not complying with certain feminist demands. Nevertheless, I respect women very much, five alone live in my immediate vicinity, that has to suffice as proof. I hope you and Alice Schwarzer will look into this simplification for me. Finally, I got support from the language expert Wolf Schneider. «What a ridiculous inconvenience it can lead to if we consistently meet the feminist demand The job description on N. Rundfunk provided a good example of this. It works like this: The director appoints his or her deputy.

I hope for your understanding, thank you very much.

A little more heart

by Enno Bunger

If you look at it that way and look at the people.

how they despise themselves?

what their looks?

what are you so tired of?

what does she look like?

why do they look so gloomy and unhappy?

Where are the good thoughts the hope for more?

why do we make our lives so difficult?

Is it really impossible to love yourself?

is it really necessary to bend yourself?

Even in the middle of spring, you only see autumn.

All you need: a little more heart a little more heart.

A little more heart.

Life is a gift, come pack it up and take it out

why don't you try it every day something completely new?

To be able to be a child again to jump over shadows hug some trees dance, laugh and sing.

Don't lose hope please don't give up!

Don't stop dancing, don't hold up the sky

Make your dreams come true.

you have to go through thick and thin,

over barbed wire fences, by waves and wind.

Everything we need: just a little more heart.

Everything we need: just a little more heart.

Everything we need: just a little more heart.

Everything we need: just a little more heart.

A little more heart.

A few warm words to slow down

This time it all starts in Wurzburg. An accident. I did not consciously create the scenario. I'm now sitting on the train to Munich and after a short train stop I continue to my destination. The day before I performed in Hanover. Now I lean back and relax and let my thoughts wander.

For weeks I had been trying to get something down on paper for my book manuscript, but I couldn't start writing, even though I noticed that my time was slowly getting tight. (The play on words at this point is not intended either, but it just fits perfectly. At first I wanted to take it out, but after the second reading it came back in. Automatically. Because it's just so beautiful.) The beginning is always the hardest part. I just couldn't find the right way to start - and that is precisely what is particularly important. Every author is terrified of disappointing his readers right from the start. Now, on the drive from Hanover to Munich - shortly before Würzburg - came the flash of inspiration to prevent this. At last. The crucial twist. Completely out of nowhere. Well, that's not entirely true either. My flash was triggered by a song. That just made it clear what was moving me the most right now. It wasn't just any song that did it, it was one of my all-time favorites: It's a Jason Mraz song.

Be that as it may, I heard the music, looked into the landscape that was now very familiar to me. I think I know every tree that stands on German railway lines by now. As so often, I linger on my thoughts. This time I think of my last birthday, the thirty-seventh. It wasn't a very nice birthday: I had to see a doctor in the morning because of a palpitations. I think thirty-seven is too early to come to the doctor with something like that. My GP examined me and found that I was otherwise physically in excellent shape. My problem originated in my head, he just said. All of this happened because of that. And that for me! And when I am the expert for it and should know what goes on in my mind, including mine.

I think it was the writer Michael Ende who once said that the signpost only shows the way, but that he doesn't have to go it himself. I always thought that I had my thoughts very well under control, that I was in control of the situation and that I knew everything about myself. And now that.

My family doctor asked me if I was currently traveling a lot. I then explained to him that I was doing a tour, giving a lot of lectures, and had only spent a day or two at home for a long time. Then he asked me if I slept through the night. "I have three children," I simply replied, "and when I'm on tour I'm often busy late into the night."

Then he grinned at me and told me the following story: During a Himalayan expedition, after three days, the Sherpas refused to continue walking out of the blue. The British clients were very upset about it. Because the group had progressed faster than originally planned, and the British wanted to extend this lead further. Still, the Sherpas insisted and didn't move an inch. They sat there and refused. Without giving reasons.

The clients tried it with good persuasion and countless arguments. "Are you too tired to keep walking?" - «No.» - «Do you have physical problems? Is the luggage too heavy? " - «No.» - «Do you want more money? We'll pay you a reward if you just keep walking! " - "No thanks." The Sherpas stayed seated and drank their tea. Then finally her explanation: "We ran a distance that we normally cover in five days, in only three days - our bodies are here now, but we have to take a break so that our souls can follow!"

A smart man, my doctor. He didn't give me any medication, just this story with me. It was one of my nicest birthday presents. And she changed me. It became clear to me that even the best thoughts and all the knowledge that one can acquire about them will not really help us if we don't take the time to let them work. So I was sitting there at the doctor's, and although I have the most beautiful job in the world, a family that always supports me, supports me in everything, and although I have been in excellent health so far, I was not doing well. There was one single factor that was wrong in my life, but it had weight: I was no longer in control of my time. I had become a victim of my demands and no longer the doer, but the driven one.

One more time I asked myself how external influences can make us do things that we really don't want to do. I now really know many methods to influence the thoughts of others and also my own. Why didn't that work at the moment? And yet: I think that's the only reason I was able to pull the rip cord at the right moment. For a long time I had said yes to projects that I really didn't want to do and hadn't noticed the vicious circle I was getting into. This question then brought me to the subject of this book - the hopefully brilliant conclusion to my thinking trilogy - and to the central aspects: Which methods influence us? How do we influence others and how can we protect ourselves from manipulation attempts by our fellow human beings?

Now I'm going to do something I've never done before: I'll tell you a magic trick. A pretty good one. With this trick a youth leader once managed to give me sleepless nights. That was in the summer of 1986. Shortly before that, my brother had passed away. It was actually not a good time. Perhaps that is precisely why my vacation with him in the French Sevennes was so important to me and - as it turned out to be much later - for my entire life.

At that time I became more and more enthusiastic about magic. So I was all the more delighted when I got to know him, an expert in card tricks. He was really good at it. His name is Jörg Roth. I haven't heard from him in over twenty years. Nevertheless, I often think of the weeks together and a particularly nice experience.

I would like to let you in on the trick he used to best deceive me. Perhaps you'd like to practice it and amaze someone with it just as much as he did me back then.

The ultimate card trick, here it is: It was in the tent camp on a beautiful sunny summer morning. We sat under a tree after breakfast and played cards. Suddenly Jörg said to me: "Just take a card from the deck and look at it carefully." It was the seven of hearts. Then I should pick up the deck of cards in front of me somewhere, put my card on the picked part on top and put the rest of the game on top. Now I was allowed to shuffle the playing cards. After I finished, he looked at me seriously. "I have no idea which card you chose, and I also don't know where your card is in the pile. Finding the right card is really difficult, isn't it? For this reason I have three free attempts, agree? " - "Of course," I replied.

He fanned out the game, picked up and showed me the bottom card. It wasn't her. He took the card out of the game and placed it face up on the floor in front of me. "Well, I still have two tries." Again he looked at the playing cards. He showed me the wrong cards twice in a row. Finally, on the floor in front of me, there were three cards in a small pile. The seven of hearts was not there.

Again he showed me the three cards on the floor one after the other and laid them out in a row in front of me. Now I was allowed to choose one of the three. He conspiratorially pushed her towards the others. He looked at me intently and said I chose the seven of hearts. Hammer! Then he asked me to turn the card over in front of me. I freaked out. The card had changed: it was my seven of hearts.

Wow, that was awesome. I had seldom been duped so pleasantly before. How did he do it? A few months later, he told me the trick. He is a prime example of the art of influencing. All you need is a deck of cards and a teammate. By the way, you always need it when doing magic! It is so difficult to amaze yourself.

Leave the deck of cards as is before the trick, or shuffle the cards if you want. Then take it back, fan it with the back side up and ask the person opposite to choose a card. Make sure it remembers the card too! Don't underestimate this advice. There is nothing more stupid than when the other player no longer knows which card he had at the end. I speak from experience. You work hard for minutes towards the grand finale and ask: "Which card did you choose?" The answer: "Um ... uh ...?"

While your viewer is looking at their card, place the rest of the cards in your left hand, backside up. Once he's done and looking at you again, use your right hand to lift about half of the stack in your left hand. Hold these cards with your thumb on one narrow edge and your middle and ring fingers on the other. Show the cards in your left hand to your spectator. Now comes the first trick: turn your right hand slightly in your wrist and point your right index finger at the cards in your left hand and ask: "Put your card back here." With this gesture and these words, look at the cards in your right hand. You will see the bottom card in the pile of your right hand, it really catches your eye.

If your spectator has now placed his card on the pile in his left hand, position the cards from your right hand on the pile as well. This gives you a big head start, because you know the map above the selected one. It is also called a guidance map. A fine thing, but unfortunately the strategy is already well known. For this reason, you now use a super good feint: you hand the deck of cards to your viewer and let them shuffle. I'm serious. Now just keep calm. You have to make sure, however, that your teammate does not mix the card game as perfectly as an American poker pro, but like a mediocre Bavarian sheep's head player. In technical jargon: There must be no ripple mixing, you have to stick to overhand mixing. You can do this by doing the mixing motion with your hands while asking him to do the same. If you don't trust the roast, just mix it yourself. The likelihood that the master card and the selected card are separated from each other when mixing overhand is very low. There is a small risk, but that's what makes things really exciting, doesn't it?

Now take the cards back and take your time to look through them. Fan the cards in front of you and find your guidance card. The card below is the selected one. But you don't take them out of the game just yet. You take any other card, put it on the bottom of the game and show it to your spectator. He will of course say that this is not his card. Now simply turn the cards down - the back is facing up - peel off the bottom card and place it on the table.

Now fan out the cards in front of you again and search specifically for the selected card, i.e. the one under your guide card. When you have found the card you have chosen, place another card on it and remove the cards so that the spectator's card is second from the bottom in the game. Any other card is in front of the chosen card. You should now be holding the game in your left hand. Turn the whole thing with the picture side, the front, towards your viewer and ask him if the card you just showed was his. Of course he will say no. His card is exactly under the card you just showed him. Now turn the game with your left hand parallel to the table. Now two things happen at the same time: First, your right hand approaches your left hand. At the same time, the middle finger and ring finger of the left hand pull the bottom card back a few millimeters. This movement cannot be seen from above. When your right hand has reached the cards in the left, it does not draw the bottom card but the second from the bottom out of the game and places it face down on the table, exactly on the card that is already there.

You have now placed the chosen card face down on the table in front of your viewer. He has no idea about it, however. This handle is also called loops in technical jargon. The nice thing about it: Your teammate thinks you don't know his card yet. But you know both about the map and its position - even more, you have already placed it on the table in front of his eyes. You look as innocent as a deer - I love moments like this. Finally, you put any card from the game down again, show it and place it on top of the other two cards that are already on the table. You can now put away the other playing cards.

Let's summarize again: On the table there are three cards on top of each other with the backs facing up. The middle one is that of the other player, which he does not know because you are a clever rascal, which he does not expect.

Now comes the ruse that beamed me away completely in the tent camp: You take the three cards from the table with the back side up in your left hand. The fingers grip the game on the long sides, the thumb is opposite. Now briefly show the bottom card - emphasize that it is not the other player's card - and place it - at least that's what you show - face down on the table.

Attention: grind again. That means you don't actually put the card shown on the table, but the viewer's card! Now of the two remaining cards in your left hand, you take one in your right. The other remains in the left. Next, briefly show both cards at the same time. In doing so, you say hypocritically: "And it wasn't and it wasn't, was it?" Don't look at the cards, look your fellow player in the eye. Believe me: if you do this skillfully and with an innocent air, no one will notice that you have shown a card twice! It also helps to choose cards with numbers for them if possible. Face cards and aces are too conspicuous. Better take sixes, fours, or eights.

There are now three cards in a row on the table. The middle one is that of the viewer. However, he thinks you are on the wrong track and has no idea what is really going on here. Now comes the next feint: you give your viewer the feeling of being able to choose freely. In reality, however, you are only always reacting to what he is doing. I'll show you what I mean.

Have your viewer point to two cards on the table. Now there are two options: He points to the two outer ones. Bingo! In that case, just put them aside. The middle card - his chosen one - is left over. He points to one of the two outer cards and then to the middle one. Doesn't matter either. Now put away the card that is left over, i.e. the outer one. Then ask him to slip a card to you. If that is the chosen card, the other one goes away. Should he push the card you did not choose, calmly pick it up and put it aside.

Do you notice what's going on right now? Exactly: No matter what the viewer does, you act as if that were exactly part of your selection process and proceed in such a way that you get to your goal. Be very relaxed and flexible. The method is very simple. However, in order to use them inconspicuously, the presentation has to be practiced and run smoothly. Incidentally, you can increase your chances of a direct hit if you point to the two outer cards yourself when asked to show two cards.

Be that as it may: After this procedure, there is now only one card on the table, namely that of your fellow player. Ask him to look deep into your eyes and think about his card. After you have focused on him, name him the correct card. I already told you that you have to remember the correct card until the end, right? After the first amazed look, ask him to turn the card on the table ... Have a glass of water - or a cognac -

ready, your viewer will need one or the other now.

If you are now wondering why I explain this trick in the preface: Very simple - I want to reward those who take the trouble to read it. Because only very few do that. There is a lot of valuable information in the foreword. By the way, the idea of hiding a small pearl in the foreword came from the English card artist Guy Hollingworth. He did it that way in his book "Drawing Room Deceptions". I found the idea wonderful.

So that no one who actually wanted to skip the foreword stumbles over my beautiful stolen idea at the last glimpse of it - that would be unfair to the hardworking - I leave a little text to confuse the lazy, something from «Wikipedia »Literally quoted and wonderfully boring as usual the prefaces. If you've been an honest reader of the foreword, you can stop here and start with the first chapter. Thank you very much. Really, nothing more here. It's not a stupid trick. Promised.

According to the classic analysis of the game, in the prisoner's dilemma, which is only played once, the only rational strategy for a player interested in his own well-being is to confess and thereby betray his fellow prisoners. Because through his decision he cannot influence the behavior of the fellow player, and regardless of the decision of the fellow player, he is always better off if he does not cooperate with the fellow prisoner himself. This analysis assumes that the players only meet once and that their decisions cannot influence subsequent interactions. Since this is a real dilemma, this analysis does not result in any clear instructions for action (prescriptive statement) for real interactions that correspond to a prisoner's dilemma. "

I invite you to use this book as your break and opportunity to break out of everyday life. With it you can withdraw into your own world - and above all: take enough time for everything!

Tampering with the front door

When I was eighteen I lived alone in my own apartment. One day the doorbell rang and a man in his mid-twenties was standing in front of it. He asked if I would answer a few questions, and it didn't take long. I agreed and he started to tell me something and then asked, "Would you help a former offender if he were safely cleansed?" - «Of course I would!» - Then he wanted to know if I had anything against East Germans. - «How do you come up with something like that? All people are the same », was my spontaneous answer. Whether I am interested in what is currently going on in the world. "Of course, after all, I'm an open-minded citizen." Whether I am equally interested in the various reports. "Of course, you can't get enough further education."

So far he had already set up four traps and armed them. I had no idea what was actually going on and was completely unprepared for his closing words. «I come from the new federal states. I am a former offender. I have served my imprisonment and I deeply regret my actions. " He is currently on the way to pull himself out of the mess by his own head of hair in order to find his way back on the right path. I could really help him with that, he assured him. He sold subscriptions to numerous magazines. Since I am obviously very interested in world affairs and would also be extremely helpful, I would certainly help him without hesitation and buy a subscription from him. The trap snapped shut, and in no time at all I had subscribed to the Stern, the Hörzu and the Spiegel. I even had a good feeling about it for a few seconds. It wasn't until a day later that I realized I had been manipulated.

This dog probably didn't even come from East Germany, and I would never know whether he really was a criminal who had been convicted. On the one hand I felt used, on the other hand I was fascinated by how brazen I had been manipulated. Today I manipulate people myself in order to earn a living, but those affected are always in a better mood afterwards than before and know what is happening to them. On the one hand I felt used, on the other hand I was fascinated by how brazen I had been manipulated. Today I manipulate people myself in order to earn a living, but those affected are always in a better mood afterwards than before and know what is happening to them. On the one hand I felt used, on the other hand I was fascinated by how brazen I had been manipulated. Today I manipulate people myself in order to earn a living, but those affected are always in a better mood afterwards than before and know what is happening to them.

In the end, I was simply tricked into doing something unsolicited outside dictated by a handful of well-functioning psychological tricks. I was influenced, yes, manipulated outright. The perfidious thing about it: I had no idea what was happening at that moment. This is one of the typical characteristics of these simple manipulation techniques. This is not just about influencing people, it is also about using tricks to force the people concerned to do something unnoticed. This is exactly what makes this method so scary. I've been into tricks for most of my life. And yet I fell for the peddler. Well, I was young and he needed the money.

What exactly happened here? How did he do that? How do manipulators even proceed today to achieve their goal? And what different methods are there to induce others to do what you want yourself? I found these questions so exciting that when I was nineteen I even went on a coffee trip with my school friends to see what perfect manipulations look like in practice. We had registered as a «bowling club all nine» in order to stay undercover as much as possible until departure. That day was an experience that I still draw from today. My conclusion: each of us has been influenced to our disadvantage in many ways. The means by which this is possible and in which areas it is particularly manipulated - that's what this book is about.

Manipulation is so scary to most of us because it creeps up on us like radiation that can make us sick. Even if you know of its existence and can define it - it is often difficult to defend yourself against it. One thing is certain: manipulation is always a suggestion. In my opinion, suggestion is an incredibly strong, but neutral force. It is neither good nor bad. It is always up to whoever masters it, and how he uses it is important. The manipulator has chosen the dark side of suggestion and uses it exclusively for his own benefit, regardless of what his action means for the other. If that were different, the manipulator could also play with open cards, right? But of course he doesn't. He uses his methods in secret. Like a magician, too, by the way. However, he immediately tells his audience that there is a secret.

But what methods did my peddler use? Well, you will find out exactly that in this book. Furthermore, on the way to the last page of the book you will get to know a lot of other suggestion and manipulation methods, because I illuminate the phenomena "manipulation" and "suggestion" from many different perspectives.

Johann Wolfgang von Goethe once said: "If you miss the first buttonhole, you will not be able to button it up." So let's start from scratch.

Rapport, the most beautiful connection in the world

So you're looking at this book right now and want to read about rapport? And that's why I begin the chapter with these very words in the heading - simply because they perfectly serve the purpose that I intended here. In this way, I can establish a connection with you through the medium of the "book". I'll pick you up right where you are. And - no matter what you think, no matter how old or young you are, whether male, female, tall, small, whatever - there is no doubt about one thing: you are looking at this book and reading. So my first attempt to get in touch was successful. I could also put it in the words of Henry Ford: "To be successful, you have to accept the other person's point of view and see things through their eyes." And slowly I can start

How important it is to see the world through the eyes of others is shown by a beautiful story in which exactly that pretty much went wrong. I heard it at a university lecture. She served as a good example of deep cultural differences.

In the 1980s, the World Health Organization (WHO) launched a large-scale advertising campaign in Pakistan to encourage newborn mothers to give milk to their infants. Because a lot of languages and dialects are spoken in this country, those responsible decided to make their message clear with three pictures: The first picture, the one on the left, shows a crying, sick baby. The middle photo showed a child drinking milk from a bottle, and on the far right you could see that a full baby was doing really well because it looked really neat. He beamed happily at the viewer. What was very stupid, however, was the fact that people in Pakistan read from right to left. You just hadn't thought of that. So if you look at advertising through the eyes of a Pakistani mother, you see the exact opposite of what a person sees in Europe. The message for a Pakistani is: If you have a healthy child and you give him milk, he will get sick. The world is what we think it is. You already know this formula from the other books. It applies here once more.

The fact that one should see the world through the eyes of the other turns out to be indispensable in many cases. This fact forms the basis of every successful contact and communication, and it also has a name: Rapport. In this context, the word has nothing to do with a military report or a general report. It is used here in a different sense, in its original sense, because it comes from French and means "relationship" or "relationship". However, it has no sexual impression, but rather describes a relationship or a relationship in general. That means: you always have to build rapport, a relationship, with another person before you can assume that he will even want to listen to you. Fortunately, this is usually very easy.

Suppose you come into contact with someone who is immediately very likeable to you. It expresses itself in a particularly distinguished way. You are impressed. And believe it or not, in no time you will match your language to the person who comes across so well to you. It works the other way too. If the other person curses constantly, you also start to lower your language level.

However, since the other person also wants to adapt to your language level, the language levels will eventually meet roughly in the middle. At best, when both harmonize very well. Or it all ends in a little game of power and influence.

Now that I've found out, I'm no longer at all surprised that my children swear after they watch me hang a lamp or try to assemble a cupboard from a Swedish furniture store. The phenomenon was investigated in 2002 by Professors Kate G. Niederhoffer and James W. Pennebaker at the University of Texas at Austin with the help of a large-scale study. They named it "Linguistic Style Matching" or "LSM", so they called it "Adaptation of language levels". Niederhoffer and Pennebaker even claimed: "When two people start a conversation, they speak the same way within a few seconds." In order to arrive at this finding, extensive experiments were carried out with students. If the task was formulated very formally, the answer was also formal. If the task was given colloquially, the students' explanations also contained loose formulations. Interestingly, the particularly well-graded responses, those of women and those of students with high socioeconomic status, were particularly adapted.

The researchers also examined the correspondence of famous people such as Sigmund Freud and Carl Gustav Jung. Their result: At the time when the writers understood each other best and expressed their friendship, the linguistic style also showed the most similarities. Even after you have watched a film, your language level will be the same as that of the main actor.

And also after reading this book, your language level will have adapted to my writing style - don't worry, I stay clean most of the time.

The study concludes with a very practical conclusion: the more harmonious the dialogues are conducted between two people, the happier the conversation partners are. This method could even serve as an indicator of happiness in marriage. Mind you: This is not about the content (the words), but about the language level. As you can see, there is a lot of power and impact in the report. And all of this just happens unconsciously!

If you want to consciously control or direct your language level, then simply think about how the other person would like to communicate. React flexibly and let it determine the course of events. That doesn't mean that you have to give up on yourself and please the other person. But on the contrary. You just adapt to his preferences. And remember: We only communicate a fraction purely on the content of a statement. Gestures, facial expressions and undertones determine the meaning and effect of our words much more than pure content. In addition to the content level, numerous other forces also prevail: speed of speech, volume, tone of voice, pauses, sounds such as sighs, laughter, to name just a few examples. Incidentally, non-verbal communication is not just wordless, but also works mostly unconsciously. Our unconscious actions while we are talking to each other therefore play a key role in ultimately fine-tuning a statement.

I usually just greet my audience with the words: "Good evening." I admit it's not really original, but I've had good experiences with this type of opening so far. Because the pure content of my statement, my wish in this case, is also not so decisive. Rather, my behavior as I pronounce these words determines how my audience will perceive them. Do I say the greeting cheerfully because I am happy that it is starting now, or do I pray it down bored? Do my shoulders hang slack or am I standing in front of the audience? All of this adds to the impact of my statement. Paul Watzlawick has already put it in a nutshell: "You cannot not not communicate."

Every action or omission in a communication has the character of a message. Paul Watzlawick calls this on the one hand the content aspect and on the other hand the relationship aspect. Let us let the Grand Master speak again personally: «If you examine what every message contains, its content turns out to be primarily information ... At the same time, every message contains another aspect that is much less obvious, but just as important. namely an indication of how your sender would like the recipient to understand it. So it defines how the sender sees the relationship between himself and the recipient, and in this sense is a personal statement. We find a content and a relationship aspect in every communication. "

In rapport, you communicate on both levels in such a way that the other person not only hears what you say, but also what you mean. You're just closer to him. It will then be easier for the person you are talking to because he does not have to try to "translate" your statement into his world.

The matter has another advantage, namely that your counterpart will find you sympathetic. You are still reading how important that can be.

It is recommended to establish rapport by observing the other closely and adapting your own behavior to the behavior of the other person. The following parameters are available for this. Here again in the overview:

- Posture and gestures,

- Volume and speed of speaking,

- Breathing rhythm and

- Undertone (paraverbal information).

Undoubtedly, all of these aspects are important for smooth communication at all levels, and they can be used specifically for optimization.

Let's look specifically at how you can build rapport with your interlocutor. Let's start with posture and gestures. Here it is very easy: just imitate the person you are talking to. Pay close attention to his posture. Recognize how he is holding his arms, what he is doing with his hands, how he is bowing his head, etc. This is exactly how you behave from now on. Then when the other moves their arm, do the same. At the same speed. There are two types of approach here.

Which method you use depends on whether the person you are speaking to is next to you or facing you. Assuming you are facing the person in question, move your right arm as they move their left. So you behave like the mirror image of your counterpart. This is why the procedure when one person assimilates himself to the other is also called "mirroring". If you are sitting next to the person, move your left arm as soon as they move their left arm. This more intensive variant is called matching. If you use this too obviously, however, then the person you are talking to will not open up, but only think that you do not have all the slats on the fence. So be careful!

It can be observed and proven: When people are completely on the same wavelength, then they strive to adjust to the partner. Take a look at couples newly in love. They like to move at the same pace, often adopt exactly the same posture and use the same volume at which they talk to each other. You still have to be very careful if you want to take advantage of this matching. You now know the technology, but you can imagine how much sensitivity you need if you really want to convince a stranger with it.

Just imagine that you notice a salesperson starting to mirror you. When you cross your arms, then suddenly he does too. As soon as you shift your weight from one leg to the other, it will do the same, etc. The moment you recognize the technology, it is no longer effective, but ineffective, and you think to yourself: "Wait a minute, it does me about straight after? Does he want to manipulate me afterwards? " From that moment on, your basic trust will be shaken and you will no longer give your counterpart a chance because you have become skeptical for good reason. And you are probably right!

So, in your own interest, proceed very gently, because mirroring is on the one hand effective, but one of the easiest methods of influencing to discover. If you use it incorrectly, you can only achieve the opposite. But it's something completely natural, and it often happens all by itself. Then the effect comes across best.

You can see it when an adult is talking to a toddler. Even university professors lapse into baby language here and thus imitate the child's behavior. Just lying down and kicking would be a little more effective, if a little exaggerated.

When mirroring postures, it is best to start with little things and build everything up slowly and gradually to perfection. At the beginning you can use similar gestures and don't have to mirror them exactly yet. These similar gestures are called "representative gestures" in technical jargon. Assuming the other crosses their arms, just place the right hand on top of the left arm. So you follow him with a similar and weakened gesture, the effect is effective because the action is only noticed indirectly.

A second variant consists in "mirroring over a cross". In doing so, you do not imitate the gesture of your conversation partner at the same time, but you wait about half a minute and then carry it out with a time delay. Even here, your counterpart will subconsciously have the impression that you are on the same wavelength without noticing anything.

Another subtle effect of the procedure is the speed with which the other person moves. Here, too, you can adjust your movements. It starts with shaking hands. With a slow person, you can take more time to reach out your hand than with a world champion in kickboxing. Last but not least, one advantage here is that you have to watch your counterpart closely. As a result, you are focused with him and in the here and now. This alone makes him feel pleasantly noticed and senses that you are interested in him and his statements. So you are not only closer to the person, but you also sharpen your powers of observation. Over time you will get better and better and you may even discover completely new aspects of your fellow human beings and tune in to them unnoticed. In this way you get the best for yourself - and perhaps also for your counterpart - out of every conversation.

I definitely want to mention a special case of mirroring: Suppose you notice that your counterpart is adopting a defensive position, crossing your arms or crossing your legs. Should you imitate the defensive posture as well? Opinions differ here. Some say it should be mercilessly mirrored through, others say that in this case you should rather adopt an open posture. As is so often the case, there is no blanket right or wrong here. It just depends. If a conflict is really noticeable in the air, then a defensive posture could give your interlocutor the impression that you are also insisting on your opinion, and the rigid posture is reinforced. In that case, you should prefer a different and more open body language and focus on other means such as speaking pace and speed. However, if you only hear one signal with which the other person is moving at a distance - for example, your arms crossed in front of your upper body - then you can record it calmly. And you should always keep in mind: Perhaps the gesture is not meant as a defense, but simply comfortable for the person - or they are cold.

As an artist, mirroring is part of my daily bread. Whenever I have a spectator on stage, I put myself in his position. In the best case scenario, mentally, I actually become almost one with him - the feeling is not easy to describe. It's a feeling of togetherness, and that feels good to both of us. Even if only I know what is going on, my counterpart on stage spontaneously and automatically feels comfortable thanks to the harmony that I create. This alone enables me to empathize with it extremely well and get an impression of how it feels, how it thinks and knows how it will behave.

So I gently adjust my breathing rhythm and posture to his and imagine myself standing on stage in the place of the audience and try to look at myself through the audience's eyes. I become that person for a brief moment. I imagine what she is feeling and thinking right now. Sometimes I also express what is on my mind at the moment. The result is usually "magical" in the truest sense of the word. This exercise is based on the principle "All is one". If you try this approach, you will feel exactly what I mean. So I not only gently reflect the physical characteristics, but also the mental ones. The result works like pure magic for everyone involved.

From Pacen and Leaden

If at some point in the course of the encounter you feel that you are communicating with the other person on the same wavelength, then you can go one step further. The progress is that you move from just mirroring to really leading the other. First of all, you see if he unconsciously follows your gestures and your speed at some point. You picked the other up at that moment and you can now lead them anywhere. If you can observe him really well and then maybe even pick up on the other person's vocabulary and behavior, this is also called "pacing", which means something like "going at the same pace" at this point. Before I can jump on a moving train, I first have to reach the same speed as the moving locomotive.

So you have now imperceptibly picked up the other person, they feel more comfortable in your presence and are very familiar with you. What's next? With the Leading. In this case, that means something like "leading". So you guide your counterpart to where you want them to go. We all know the phenomenon: There are people with infectious happiness. Their presence alone increases their own good mood. Most of the time, these people are unaware of their effect, but they experience a lot of sympathy.

The following example shows how you can use this strategy: Let's assume you have an acquaintance who is not in a good mood. There is no really serious reason for his depression. It's just a rainy day, the wrong football club has won, or his daughter came home the day before with a guy who, at sixteen, wears corduroy trousers and a bow tie. You can help this acquaintance with your mood. Just build rapport as described and start pacing.

These English terms get on my nerves, too, but you already know what I mean. When you notice that rapport has been established, change your posture and watch whether the other person is following you. If it follows you, adopt a more open and positive posture. Smile, keep your back straight, and look straight ahead - definitely not down. Check carefully whether your friend with the corduroy son-in-law is following you. As soon as you lose it at any point, simply go back to the starting point where you had consciously mirrored it in order to create rapport again. According to the motto: two steps forward and one step back.

Since the energy follows the attention, his mood will certainly improve with the new posture, because parallel to a posture that expresses: "I'm fine", it is very difficult to think, "I'm bad."

I have already described why this is so in my book "I know what you think". There is one exception, however: when someone is really sad. We all have the right to be dejected from time to time and then legitimately fight back. You know: In bad moments, all beautiful sayings are useless. In grief, we need enough time and energy to process the cause of the grief. We are right to react indignantly if we do not feel respected by the other. But if your friend only feels a little blues, the method is very useful.

So far we have only limited ourselves to the aspect of "posture" when it comes to pacing and leading. But there is much more to consider. Pacing and leading can be implemented and used in many forms of influencing. As a parent, for example, you can still use this method to give your children good answers to the most nonsensical suggestions. Let us take a typical discussion between father and five-year-old son that takes place practically every day in our household. It's 6.30 p.m. on Monday evening and you're at dinner. The son: "Dad, may I watch 'Ice Age' afterwards?" Father (wrong answer): "You're crazy, look at the clock. We all have to get up early tomorrow. The film lasts over an hour and a half, and you know exactly how you will be on it tomorrow if you haven't slept off.

Dear reader, I too am sometimes tempted to answer such a nonsensical question so openly, clearly and clearly. But since effectiveness is the measure of truth, I can only urgently advise you not to do it this way. In no case do not let yourself get carried away, you will not get any results. First, the answer is mercilessly harsh and potentially inappropriate, second, you tear down all bridges to possible compromises, and third, in the evening when your child asks such a question, your child doesn't, definitely doesn't know what it will be like the next morning, if it won't have slept off. Children live according to the motto: "Now is the moment of power", and that's enough.

If they are fit and in a good mood now, they just don't know that if they went to bed late they'll feel hungover the next morning. They just turn off such thoughts, if they even have them. Incidentally, just like children can filter out all disturbing frequencies of the voices of their parents and grandma and grandpa from their hearing on command. Just like annoying advice. For good reason. Let's take a look at a more suggestive and, for both sides, much more peaceful word structure.

The father now gives the correct answer: "Hm, you would like to watch something on TV. I think the idea is okay, you were really nice today. (The sentence always works, by the way, even if the dear little ones have just decorated the freshly attached wallpaper with stamps.) From me you can still look at Sandman. "

Most of the time it works so much better. This is because in the second example the child does not feel offended. No pressure is built up at which it feels called upon to react with counter pressure. Instead, the instruments "pacing" and "leading" are used. They are much gentler. In this example, the pacing lies in taking up the idea of watching television. So then I'll take my son with me and link his idea with mine. So it's not just about creating rapport through body posture, speaking speed, volume, language and breathing rate. It is also about creating consistency in terms of content - via an idea that we can take up, modify and use as a starting point for our proposal.

The unconscious raising of the arms

You need a teammate to stand in front of you.

Ask him to close his eyes and take a few deep breaths and then exhale. Once he is visibly relaxed, continue.

- Clap gently - with your hands following clockwise - seven times in a circular motion around the other person's face, neck, shoulders and chest. Then take hold of both wrists of your teammate and gently move them sideways at a 45-degree angle up to shoulder height. Hold your arms there for a while before lowering them back down.

- Please repeat this action three more times. Do exactly the same thing every time: clap seven times clockwise and then gently lift the other person's arms up, pause briefly and then lower them again.

- The fourth time, clap exactly as you did before, but this time don't raise your teammates arms up. Even though you are not touching the other player, his arms will be drawn upwards as if by invisible threads.

- A wonderful exercise in "pacing" and "leading". The exercise also shows you clearly how strongly a person responds to your suggestions and how well they are suitable for hypnosis.

Walker between the worlds

I quoted Paul Watzlawick at the beginning of this chapter. First, because it is always smart to consult the linguist, and second, because we were able to get to know two crucial levels of communication, the content and the relationship level. I cannot emphasize enough what this wealth of knowledge means to me. It has been very valuable very often. A few years ago, my coach and friend Michael Rossié casually advised me to look into this topic. Young as I was then, I thought to myself: «Logical. I already know that. What does he want from me now? " However, even then there were a few people in my life who were almost always right when they said something. He was one of them. Because of this, while I pretended to be cool and indifferent, but immediately rushed to the relevant literature as soon as I got home. And I ran into a gold mine! What I would like to bring closer to you now has served me well in numerous TV programs and interviews and is one of the foundations of my work. And I couldn't make it clearer than P. Watzlawik and would like to cite a well-known example that I would like to take from him here:

The door dilemma according to P. Watzlawick

A man is locked in a room. Two doors lead out of the room. Both are closed, but only one is really locked. There is a guard in front of every door. One of the guards always tells the truth, the other always lies. The prisoner knows that, but he doesn't know which of the guards is telling the truth and which is lying. (Because he hasn't read this book.) He's allowed to ask one of the guards a single question to find out which door leads to freedom.

What's the solution? It's quite clever: the prisoner points to one of the two doors and asks one of the two guards: "If I asked your comrade whether this door leads to freedom, what would he say?" Isn't that great? If the guard says no, the door is open, if the guard says yes, the door is locked.

The wonderful thing about this example is the fact that the solution is figured out simply by addressing the content level (is the door open or closed?) And the relationship level (between the guards and the one who doesn't lie and the one who lies) become. The detour to get one piece of information through another piece of information leads to the solution.

Believe it or not, it is often no different in real life. Imagine a man bought a sports car. A colleague speaks to him about it and asks him: "What did it cost?" This question is not just about the price, i.e. the level of information, but also, without exception, always about the relationship between the two interlocutors. Body language, facial expression and undertones will always convey the attitude of the questioner, there is no other way. Is the emphasis in the question such that it appears admiring, joyful, jealous, or indifferent? What does his face look like? What is his body signaling? The person asked cannot respond to such a request. Even if he ignores her, it's a reaction.

At this point it should not go unmentioned that we almost never use the relationship level consciously - in contrast to the content level. We mostly only enter them unconsciously. The few situations in which we consciously choose them therefore usually end unpleasant. This is why it sometimes has such a negative effect when a person reads a text who simply cannot. We'll shut down immediately. That brings us back to the report: If the accent is wrong, we usually break it off within a very short time.

I once had an economics professor whom I couldn't listen to for more than two minutes, even with the greatest effort and concentration. He came into the classroom, unpacked his papers, and began to read. He almost never looked at us students. After three events, the report broke off so severely that I stopped going and just studied at home from his book. Well-trained actors show the other extreme. They can read what they want. Because they are so intense in the text, through their facial expressions, gestures and melody, they can build rapport immediately, and we like to listen to them.

Watzlawick therefore repeatedly makes it clear that the relationship level is never consciously controlled in positive conversations. The more the attempt is made to consciously shape the relationship, the more conflictual the relationship between the interlocutors becomes. It can ultimately end in massive disputes in which the content, however, loses its meaning completely. The famous tube of toothpaste or the wrongly cooked breakfast egg ultimately lead to a major marriage crisis. You know that. Purely in terms of content, ridiculous, on the relationship level of great importance.

In this context, it is important to me to mention that rapport can only work without exception if both levels are taken into account. A sentence like: "I think this book is outstanding" can have at least five different meanings - depending on which word is emphasized. It is therefore extremely important that we always keep in mind that every communication has a content and a relationship level, with the relationship level determining the content level. Copy this sentence down, memorize it, and show it off at the earliest opportunity.

Iceberg in sight

The following example shows very clearly what I mean:

- Imagine an iceberg floating in the water. No more than twenty percent of the colossus protrudes from the water, which means that at least eighty percent floats below the surface of the water.

- Imagine that the visible tip of the iceberg is a symbol for the factual level. Everything that is invisible under the surface represents the relationship level (subtext, body language, facial expressions). To clearly show the importance of the relationship level in communication, make the following clear: Imagine two icebergs drifting towards each other and colliding. Where will they meet first? Can you see it …

I had already mentioned that the knowledge of these connections has already served me well, especially in interviews. And now that you too know the system, I can also explain to you how you can use it for yourself as a means of reporting.

Here's a case to start with: Suppose you make a suggestion to your partner. For reasons that are completely inexplicable to you, he verbally and harshly rejected it, saying, "I don't think much of that". The emphasis is aggressive and sounds annoyed. You could now stick to the content level and say, "Why? I think the proposal is very good. " Then a counter-argument will probably come back on the content level and your partner says: "Then do it, but I don't think much of it." In order to break off the report completely, you could also annoyedly say: "I'll do it too." And that's it then.

Believe me, even if you used the same posture, tone of voice, breathing rate and intonation, yes, even if you were wearing the same clothes and had the same birthday as the person you were speaking to: the report would be gone. You can use this strategy wherever you want. In business, in professional life, when shopping, it doesn't matter. The report breaks off because the error is not on the content level, but on the relationship level. And you don't crack them through confrontation. Pressure only creates counter pressure here. Fortunately, it is much easier and also more elegant.

In order to establish rapport in such a case, you just have to agree with your counterpart. Don't you think so? Yes, believe me. And before you put this book in the bin for waste paper, please read at least the next few lines. There you will find out how you can still get the curve around and make your winning argument effectively. Make yourself aware that humans are the only living creatures who die for their beliefs! If you doubt this belief, especially after it has been spoken out loud, you will always be met with a sharp wind. So, give in first. Your moment is still to come, I promise. Building rapport is always about seeing the world from the other's point of view. That does not mean, that in the end he is absolutely right. But - and this is extremely important - from his point of view he is always right. This basically means that if you were in the other person's place, you would act exactly as they did, and that is exactly what you could emphasize by first giving in and never being rigid. Your counterpart is already doing that. And it will only make you smarter.

So suppose, on a well-intentioned suggestion, you get a sentence like: "I don't think much of this", the emphasis is aggressive until it stops, then you just say: "Maybe you are right, and my suggestion is not this best. That may be. What I don't understand is why you are so pissed off about it. " Believe me, that's a real magic formula. Remember, the relationship level determines the content level!

It was probably Einstein who said: "Problems can never be solved on the same level on which they arose." If you wander between the worlds and change levels, this creates rapport. Because we can only resolve such a disturbed exchange of views on the relationship level. The chance that your interlocutor will now calmly explain to you why he presented his counter-argument so aggressively increases drastically with this approach.

I can still remember how I used this method when I first appeared on «TV total» with Stefan Raab. I was so excited before and during the show that I vomited as soon as I got back to my cloakroom. Keep your eyes open when choosing a career! The performance was anything but puke and later opened a few doors for me. But back to the topic: Stefan immediately said to me with a malicious grin: "Well, Thorsten, then show us a trick." I replied: "To be honest, I don't know for sure whether what I'm going to do is working here, because I have the impression that you are trying to fool me."

Even Stefan Raab rowed back at that moment and said in a sense: "No, no, I just want to see a sample." So I was able to build rapport again. By the way, even if he had admitted that he wanted to fool me - the fronts would have been cleared for the audience. One magic phrase that always works in this regard is, "If I were in your place, I would think the same way" - and then just add your argument.

By the way, there is another good trick to quickly establish rapport: Get the other person to talk about themselves. There is no other topic that interests people as much as you do yourself. If you can get the other person to talk about yourself, they will have the impression that you are a very good conversationalist because you made it possible for them to do so. You can also use this opportunity to try out the "mirroring", "pacing" and "leadening" methods described here. As soon as the interlocutor can talk about himself and his attitudes, he is not consciously aware of what you are doing. He's so busy with himself.

Cancel or don't even start?

Under certain circumstances it can make sense to cut the rapport or not to let it arise in the first place. You can do this easily and gently by moving a little physically and figuratively away from the person you are speaking to, changing your pitch and choosing your words accordingly. A friendly "no thanks" usually serves its purpose quite well. In extreme cases, you should not only interrupt eye contact, but also turn your back on the person you are talking to. The report is then definitely interrupted. Remember: you don't have to accept and follow every tip in this book at the same time! But there are numerous occasions when it can be useful to break the rapport. For example:

- When concluding a sales pitch. Shortly before the contract is to be signed by the customer, it makes sense to give the buyer time to think about everything again in his own personal world. Because only then can he freely decide whether he will feel comfortable with the purchase in the end or not. This approach is particularly suitable for long-term customer loyalty - and thus for reporting.

- And: Suppose you have a boring babble in front of you that wants to verbally copy over all the information on your hard drive. What to do without looking rude Just do the opposite of everything that's advised in this chapter.

Finally, a little thing on the side: Please proceed with all of the methods described here with care. There are simply people you shouldn't be flipping over to establish rapport. For example, in a patient with Tourette's syndrome - this is a very rare disease - it would really make no sense to ape the verbal component or the physical tick. And basically: all physical disabilities are of course taboo for mirroring. Linguistic coloring also only makes sense to support the rapport if you really speak the dialect. As soon as I talk to my mother on the phone, for example as a Saarland native, my wife suddenly hears who is at the other end. I immediately fall into the tones of home, because I associate them with my home and see them as completely normal, as soon as I meet people from the region. However, it would not occur to me to speak Saarland in Munich or - even worse - try to speak Bavarian. As soon as something is not really inside you and thus would never seem natural, you can never apply it credibly. After all, all power comes from within. And you are only authentic if the inside and outside match.

Let me end this chapter with a quote from Milton H. Erickson, an eminent hypnotherapist. He summed up many essential aspects of communication - also with regard to rapport: "Whenever you do something that doesn't work, stop and do something else." I think it was Einstein once again who expressed the wisdom a little differently, but meant exactly the same thing: "Only an idiot believes that if he does the same thing twice, the result will be different." Here, too, as always, effectiveness is the measure of truth. If one method does not work for a conversation partner, then just take another!

Flattering things for all situations

What is this now? I can literally hear you ask yourself this question after reading the heading. Here is my short story to explain.

Some time ago I was invited to his show by M. Lanz. The topics on that day were among others «card reading» and «astrology». To be honest, I'm not an expert in either of these fields. But I am very familiar with methods that make my audience believe that I know everything about my counterpart and that I can describe their thoughts, their character and their living conditions very precisely.

That is exactly what astrologers and fortune-tellers do too. Before you read the story, I would like to make one thing clear: I have no objection to any of these arts. Both card reading and star reading are topics that many intelligent people have dealt with very seriously and in depth. For example, in India, a country where astrology has a very long tradition, there is a so-called palm leaf library.

It represents one of the last great mysteries of the country. Legend has it that astrologers who were particularly talented in the media once wrote down the personal fates and lives of millions of people on palm leaves. Lives were recorded because the prophetic monks knew that sooner or later the souls concerned would come back to the library. However, there is one catch: There is only a library in Chennai, as far as we know. You have to register there a year in advance in order to be able to see your palm leaf. There is no waiting time for the other palm leaf libraries - but nobody knows exactly where they are ...

The records record people's past, present, and future lives. For some it is a real help in life, for others it is pure slapstick. What I mean by that: I give lectures and entertain people. In doing so, I use methods with which I give the impression that I can fathom their innermost being. Among other things, I use a special method that I will introduce to you in this chapter. It has nothing to do with mysticism, only with psychology. But that doesn't mean that the mystical doesn't really exist. It just means that mysticism is not sought in this case. That's all. This is not a rating. Because here too - as always - it depends on the individual case.

On the one hand, there are many hypocrites with excessive self-confidence among the esoteric and mystics, on the other hand, one can also find enlightened scientists among them. That doesn't really mean anything, except that there are people with too big egos everywhere.

Back to my experiment with M. Lanz. Before the broadcast was recorded, I claimed to be a very well-known and recognized astrologer and to be able to use the exact date of birth to create a precise character analysis and, as a result, a horoscope for the people in question. My offer was to write such a profile for six participants. They should already be able to read it on the show. They then had to say how precisely the analysis described them. The result was clear: on a scale from one to ten, none of them gave me less than seven points. One lady even thought that I had hired a private detective in her case, because that was the only way to get such personal insights.

The actor Armin Rohde was also on the show and also got his horoscope. He quoted a passage that - as he emphasized - described one hundred percent inside. So it was a complete success. But you may already guess how the resolution will turn out. I now asked those involved to exchange their horoscopes among themselves and to read them again: All had received exactly the same text.

This test has become known under the name "Forer Experiment". If you want to know more about Forer's work: I already introduced the phenomenon in "I know what you think". Of course you are now wondering: what kind of test was that? I don't want to print the exact wording here in order to keep a little of the secret. Maybe just try it yourself. I only want to describe here how I went about writing. With my "personal" horoscope, I managed to build up such a strong report over six A4 pages that the people concerned would have believed me almost everything afterwards - so the technology is undoubtedly very powerful and at the same time dangerous if you read it wrong hands.

That's how it works!

In "I know what you think" I already described that there are seven central subject areas for each of us that we are interested in.

In order to create a feeling of closeness and rapport, you could first choose one of these areas, work on it and address it. While doing this, watch your counterpart and see whether you were able to land a hit with your guess or not.

By the way: In the "Faces" chapter, there are a few more pointers that will help you to recognize this.

- Put yourself in the shoes of the other person: Suppose you go to someone who is supposed to help you. Why are you doing this? Probably because in one of the following areas of life things are not going as you imagine. This always includes:

  - Health,

  - love (including sex),

  - money,

  - Job.

  These are the four most important. Make up the rest:

  - hopes and future,

  - Education (knowledge acquisition) and - Travel and change of location.

- Everyone is interested in these topics. Guaranteed. So it's worth keeping the list in mind.

- In addition, there is a second factor: Every person has another topic that concerns them beyond measure: themselves. Otherwise, not every daily newspaper, including the reliable, daily horoscopes would be printed. Everyone wants to find out something about themselves and their life. Because of this, you can easily establish rapport with someone by letting them talk about themselves. That's already in the book How to Make Friends. The Art of Becoming Popular and Influential »by Dale Carnegie. He gives a simple and very good tip: "Convince your counterpart that you are a fantastic conversation partner by getting them to talk about themselves. From that moment on you can listen, start mirroring and encourage him to keep talking. "

The procedure that I am giving you here has three other great advantages:

- Firstly, your counterpart never has the impression that they have been questioned.

- Second: the other person thinks you can read minds.

- Third, even if you are wrong about one thing, there is always a believable way of twisting it so that you are ultimately right. It only depends on your smartness and your rhetorical skills.

I forgot something: First, make a rough estimate of the age of the person you are talking to. Once you've sorted it out, you're good to go. The fact is that although we all think we are outstandingly unique individuals and have our own personal and our very own worries, in reality our problems are almost always typical of a certain phase of life and very predictable because they are influenced by general ones Conditions in a phase of life are influenced. An eighteen year old has other things on his mind than a sixty year old. A very extensive book was written about this phenomenon as early as the 1970s. It is by Gail Sheehy, a journalist and speaker, and is called "Passages, Predictable Crises of Adult Life".

A few years later a German translation was published with the title "In the middle of life. Coping with foreseeable crises ». You should definitely read this. Because if you know the age of a person, then with what I am going to explain to you in the next chapter you can say very accurately what concerns the person sitting in front of you. That's exactly what I tried to do in my M.

Lanz horoscope, and it obviously succeeded. The people here whose guesswork hit the mark were between thirty-five and fifty-five years old. So, let's go!

Between eighteen and thirty-five

Men between the ages of eighteen and thirty-five are interested in their careers and goals. Then comes their relationship with women. Even if you don't have a boyfriend, this topic is interesting: you definitely consider the possibilities of what it would be like to get married and start a family. At this age almost everyone has the impression that everything is going too slowly and they see their talents underestimated and not really appreciated by others. During this time, many men look for a mentor, someone who takes them under his wing and lets them share in his wisdom or gives them an insight into business life. You keep wondering whether they will lead a successful life and in which field they will continue their education or which of their skills they should better develop. As a rule, what they have learned so far is not enough. Money and reputation play a big role. The young gentlemen naturally also ask themselves where the best money can be earned and how they can get a piece of the big cake.

Women between the ages of eighteen and thirty-five either want to know whether they will meet the right person - or whether they already know him - and may already be with him. They are interested in whether they will be financially secure one day, and they wonder what they can do to achieve the highest level of security and protection for their children and themselves. In addition, there is the important aspect of further human relationships for them. So they think hard about how they can present themselves as attractively as possible. Why they are having trouble with a particular person or matter.

By the age of thirty they feel the emerging concern about getting older and think about their role in the family. Most marry in their late twenties or early thirties. In retrospect, you usually judge your pre-marriage relationships as negative. Or at best as a good experience. They want to know if they can get the man they want and if they will be able to retain him. Many women between the ages of twenty and thirty fear an unwanted pregnancy. Their own mother plays a big role for them - in a good or in a bad sense.

But you can also be very ambitious professionally, see men critically or loathe them or first dream of future success in life and a later marriage with the right person. But one thing applies to everyone: the future seems uncertain, and you do everything to take the right path - regardless of whether someone is more career-oriented or marriage-oriented.

Both sexes, men and women, between the ages of eighteen and thirty-five feel this: During the final years of their teenage years and early twenties, they try a lot to find themselves. During your youth you like to develop ideas, quirks and follies that are as far removed from the parents' ideas as possible in order to feel and differentiate yourself.

Outwardly, they seem self-confident, but in reality there is a clear feeling of fear behind this often excessive self-confidence. The central aim of life in this section is to look for security everywhere, to find one's role, for example in the partnership, in one's professional constellation, but also in convictions and ideologies, a home, to uncover a grid. In this phase everyone looks for like-minded people who still confirm their own attitudes and are comrades-in-arms who understand you.

This phase is characterized by a feeling of turmoil: on the one hand you want to be independent, on the other hand you need a clear feeling of security. In their twenties, everyone tries to dream their dream, which hopefully they will be able to realize one day. Professional development and relationships are essential. We try to do what we think we should. But it is often a back and forth between wanting to commit to yourself and trying out new possibilities. Most of us try on the one hand not to commit ourselves too much and to remain flexible at all times, and on the other hand we still want to stand up to ourselves and always have the certainty that we are taking the right path and following it consistently.

At thirty, we feel like we're too narrowing down on what we've already established and generally being too restrictive. We feel a second surge of vitality. Very often there is now a career change and a realignment of life goals. Often we suddenly have the feeling that we are wasting time with what we are doing. Many people of this age attend evening school or go to university again and continue their professional development or even take a completely new path.

Then, at around thirty-five years of age, you focus entirely on your job. People in this phase feel that their lifespan is slowly becoming too short to achieve all of their goals. That is why they give everything to make further progress in their careers. They really step on the gas because they think this is their last chance to make something of themselves. From this phase on, other needs outside of the job are often neglected in favor of the professional career. You will usually only become aware of them again from forty.

From thirty-five to fifty-five

Men in this phase of life want to know again. An important professional decision, a large investment, or a major project: what is paying off and what is doing well? Furthermore, they are still very intensively concerned with the question: What is still going on? What is my main goal, my dream? What can still be done now? The gentlemen wonder what has become of all their previous goals, hopes and ambitions. What happened if? What if I had made a different decision back then? What would my life be like then? These are the classic questions of life. Some wish they could start all over again. The relationship level also comes into focus. They wonder why others misunderstand or dislike them and they begin to worry about their health.

Women between the ages of thirty-five and fifty-five want to be sure that they are making the right decisions. They think about the job, finally about the wedding, their relationship with their partner and their sincerity. Some are now wondering whether they want to break out of their everyday routine and see the world. You notice the first physical problems and limitations. They begin to worry about their children, fear and wonder if - and when - the man's income will continue to rise. In addition, it may well be that during this time you question the loyalty of your partner and put it to the test. Many bury their teenage hopes and some become melancholy, if not unhappy and dissatisfied.

Both sexes now feel the same in many respects: At around forty years of age, many people change jobs and partners. The phases of life between late thirties and early forties are marked by a reassessment and possibly a change.

From around forty-five years of age, life returns to normal and the situation becomes more stable. Those who were temporarily stuck in a life crisis find a new meaning. Those who have not yet been through most likely feel an internal stagnation that needs to be resolved. It is not uncommon for men and women to have diametrically opposed goals. Women are looking for new peaks to climb, men are looking for ways to take it easy soon, and may even give up on their ambitious goals from the twenties.

From the second half of life

Men over fifty-five suddenly wonder how long they'll live. Some, whose relationship is no longer satisfactory, want to experience real love again. To be admired all over again. They think about what they could do with their money, make daring plans, but at the same time they are tormented by the thought of getting seriously ill one day. Some worry about the financial situation in old age, their living conditions after the job, and think again about whom they can trust when it comes to safeguarding their interests.

Between the ages of fifty and fifty-five men get into a kind of menopausal phase. During this time, all the emotions come up that have been suppressed for years for the sake of a career. In many cases this leads to a feeling of sadness or even despair. This phase is very difficult for the person concerned. It's like those repressed bubbles of feeling are getting bigger and bigger and are about to burst.

Women aged fifty-five and over consider whether they will remain alone if they are widows or whether they will die before their husbands if they are wives. You are wondering whether a lucrative investment is still worthwhile or whether a plan for the later years can still be implemented. You weigh everything even more carefully and always get a second opinion from the doctor. They too want to know if they will ever love properly again and what to do about feelings of sadness if they are unhappy in their relationship. Will I be as carefree as I was back then? She doesn't let go of this thought.

And men and women from the age of fifty-five feel this way: Those who have been able to process their emotions, ups and downs, reach a new level of happiness. They are confident and express their opinions very directly. You become more active and live a truly individualistic life. This life almost feels like a second youth. They may think about their impermanence, of course wondering whether they will have a serious operation at some point, but some can suppress such gloomy thoughts for a while. The idea of impermanence always triggers fear, but it only indirectly determines action.

A short history of hypnosis in 7500 characters

As soon as the word "hypnosis" comes up, most people think of mindless, distant people who are completely under the influence of a powerful person. This is usually the and first declaration that is made. The medical benefits of hypnosis only come to mind when you think twice about it. In my previous books I have avoided the term. For good reason. I did this because I had the impression that most people immediately take a negative attitude as soon as the word "hypnosis" is uttered. Indeed: it has a slightly negative aftertaste. Most people experience a reluctance and a natural defensive reaction against attacks on their independence and self-control.

Nevertheless, in my previous appearances, I never had problems asking test subjects to come on stage for hypnosis experiments. At such moments, the audience was always split into three camps: the averse, the neutral observer and the curious. The curious immediately stormed the stage and got involved in it in no time. However, all groups had one thing in common: They were fascinated by what was happening. This fascination has existed for a long time, because hypnosis already has a remarkable history to record.

Reports of the so-called "temple sleep" - an archetype of hypnosis - have come down to us from ancient times. Because in Greece the sick went to priests and lay down to sleep in the temple after introductory ablutions and rituals. Then the priests whispered suggestions in their ears to activate their self-healing powers.

The Cologne scholar Heinrich Cornelius Agrippa von Nettesheim (1486-1535) already used hypnosis and described it in his works. Back then, in the times of the Inquisition, that was not without danger. As a result, he was imprisoned as a wizard and sorcerer. But after he even cured people in prison, he was released. Lucky, it could have ended up with torn out fingernails or at the stake.

The first real hypnotist in today's sense was Franz Anton Mesmer (1734 - 1815). He came from Iznang on Lake Constance. His hypnosis experiments were so spectacular that the word "mesmerized" still stands for "banned" or "tied up" in English today. So he seems to have been a really cool dog - and also a friend of Wolfgang Amadeus

Mozart. Mesmer believed that all things are connected by a magnetic fluid. An interruption of this natural flow of energy leads to illness. As soon as he uses his "magnetic strokes" to direct the energy back into the right path, the patient can be cured. Mesmer made magical passes over the sick bodies to heal them. First with magnets, later with bare hands. He already knew in his day that show effects have a big impact. His sessions were always a sensation: he performed in purple robes and had female musicians play music on a glass harp in the background of the performances.

He had his patients sit around a tub of water with their knees pressed together. Mesmer emphasized that this way the energy, the magnetic fluid, can flow better. Iron bars with wires attached to them protruded from the vat. The participants in the session should hold these iron bars in their hands to allow the magnetic energy to pass from one to the other. During the sessions, Mesmer's very attractive assistants stroked the patients' sensitive parts of the body - some of the patients were so "mesmerized" that they got ecstatic twitches. Then the master himself appeared to calm the banished meeting participants with one of the iron rods by touching their faces, stomach area and breasts - I can only say: Keep your eyes open when choosing a career, I just shake hands with my audience. Finally, a commission was set up by the French king to examine Mesmer's treatment methods more closely.

This commission, made up of doctors and scientists, found his work unscientific. All healing successes can be ascribed to the imagination of the patient. Interestingly, the scientists were absolutely right, after all, all power comes from within ... The scientists did not care that the exaggerated theatrical presentation of the sessions led to the healing of many patients. Unfortunately, no further research was carried out in this direction at first. Instead, Mesmer's work has been banned. I think the commissioners were just jealous: they would certainly have liked to stroke the breasts of the Parisian high-society ladies with iron sticks. However, this is a pure speculation on my part.

Still, the topic continued to fascinate people. In 1819 the Portuguese Abbé Faria (1746 - 1819) found out that the trance or hypnotic state can also be brought about without fluid and solely through convincing suggestion. He simply stepped in front of the person concerned, looked them intently in the eyes and suddenly said: "Sleep!" Half of the people addressed immediately fell into a trance. Today this phenomenon is known as lightning hypnosis.

The actual term "hypnosis" was coined by James Braid (1795 - 1860), a Scottish ophthalmologist. That was in 1819. He dealt intensively with technology - with the aim of unmasking it. To his astonishment, he found that it worked. To purify his disbelief, he called the state "hypnosis", after the Greek word "hypnos" for sleep. Despite his success, Braid was also ridiculed by his colleagues.

In France, the doctor Ambroise-Auguste Liébault (1823-1904) then tested the effect of braids experiments and was able to confirm them. Hyppolite Bernheim (around 1840-1919) became aware of this and introduced hypnosis and suggestion as a treatment method in the Nancy clinic. Together with Liébault, Bernheim founded the so-called School of Nancy. That was the beginning of the scientific application of this healing method.

A short time later, the work of Sigmund Freud (1856-1939) caused a sensation. Freud himself was a student at the Nancy school. His works on psychoanalysis hit like a bomb. At that time, the method was hardly considered as a serious form of therapy. The industrial revolution was in full swing. You just had other interests. New forms of energy generation (e.g. steam engine) and the development of new machine systems (e.g. weaving machine) conquered science and technology.

But I should mention one more: Milton H. Erickson (1901 - 1980). Many people consider him a true figure of light, and he is said to have almost magical abilities. Erickson is namely the father of modern hypnotherapy. He suffered from polio and was able to use his methods to alleviate his own suffering through self-hypnosis. His approach was completely new. Instead of appearing as an authoritarian and mystical hypnotist, he withdrew as a person and did not focus on himself, but on his patients. It was precisely through this that he made hypnotherapy ripe for the modern age and received a status and a following that made Mesmer - despite his purple suits - very pale. Now we can move on to the more practical part of the phenomenon and look at what hypnosis does to us.

How does that work, put into deep sleep?

I have been asked in many of my radio and television interviews to put a person into a live trance. I have always refused to do this. I did it mainly because I knew that the words I uttered not only reach the audience in the room, but also those who are listening or watching elsewhere. I once hypnotized someone on a show. When I had finished speaking, not only was the viewer in a trance, but also the sound engineer, who had been listening to my contribution through headphones. It would therefore be highly reckless and immoral to hypnotize a person out of control without making sure who the hypnosis is reaching. On a live broadcast, hundreds of drivers would probably fall asleep on my command, as soon as I did something like that on the radio. That would make a big headline, but this is a form of PR that I'm not looking for.

By the way, just as little as I want to draw attention to the RTL jungle camp. The broadcaster asked me if I would like to travel with them. There I could eat animal testicles, get electric shocks, be locked up with slipped celebrities and be watched around the clock. Well, all of this is a very exciting psychological experiment - but I prefer to take part in it with a glass of single malt in my living room. The whole thing seems more like a mixture of the programs "Lost" and "Teletubbies". That's why I always reject something like that.

It is unimaginable that even more people would be at risk of accidentally falling into a trance if they were to appear on TV. If the conditions are mediocre, one million viewers can watch a show - and that would still be a very bad rate. Literally hundreds of thousands would be at risk of being hypnotized too. A huge amount and gigantic range for hypnotic manipulation.

Even if only a handful of this large number responded fully to the manipulation, the risk that it posed would be immense. Do you know one hundred percent, dear reader, that you wouldn't be one of them?

One of the most perfidious manipulations would be a so-called post-hypnotic command. These are instructions that are given to the viewer during hypnosis with the request to carry them out at a later point in time. I remember a hypnosis show I saw once in an amusement park. There the audience on the stage was ordered to immediately fall back into the hypnotic state, the trance, when they heard the word "super". This command was not reversed by the hypnotist. About an hour later I happened to be standing directly behind one of the hypnotized spectators in the queue for the roller coaster. He talked to his girlfriend and said in a general manner: "Don't you have any queasy feeling before the trip?" The friend said: "No, I think this will be great ...!" And jerk Her friend was in a trance again and was no longer responsive. The lady at the cash register immediately (!) Dialed the number of the hypnotist by heart. He came immediately and woke the young man up again. The command was only then deleted. The cashier said it had happened the third time this week!

What exactly happened there for the third time in a week? Well, there is a definition in Kurt Tepperwein's book "The High School of Hypnosis". Accordingly, hypnosis according to Dr. L. Chertok a "temporary state of altered attention in the patient, a state in which various phenomena can arise spontaneously or in response to verbal and other stimuli. These phenomena include a change in consciousness and memory as well as an increased sensitivity to suggestions and thoughts in the patient that are not familiar to him in his usual state of mind. Among other things, phenomena such as anesthesia, paralysis, muscle rigidity and vasomotor changes can be caused and suppressed in the hypnotic state. " In my opinion, the important thing is

This definition also explains why I pay so much attention to the subject of "hypnosis" in this book: In this form of being we have an increased susceptibility to suggestions. This is manipulation at the highest level. Sensible people hug a broomstick on stage, play an invisible piano, and eat an onion thinking it's an apple. Of course, I'm only talking about show hypnosis here, I know my way around better, I have learned about it.

All of this may seem extremely questionable and uneventful - it is always fascinating. And with show hypnosis in particular, I learned one thing: Hypnosis has a very strong effect. If it works! One could also say again: "Effectiveness is the measure of truth." Nevertheless, at my performances I met some people who absolutely wanted to be the center of attention and just played. An experienced hypnotist immediately recognizes such actors and sends them back to their place.

Would something like that work through a book? Well, strictly speaking, you are in a trance state every time you are completely absorbed in reading a book and forget about everything around you. Which, I hope, happened when your eyes slid over the lines of my book. Because while you read my words, you notice how you - quite incidentally - become more and more calm and relaxed. You let go of everything else because you need all your concentration to read.

Let's do a little test. It will work the first time for most of you. By the way, with the help of this test I was able to start my television career. This number was part of my TV show "The Mind Reader" in January 2005 and was a resounding success.

The magnetic fingers of a hand

- Sit down and relax. Place this book next to you so that you can still read from it comfortably and have both hands free.

- Now, please cross the fingers of both hands, hold them in front of you and press the fingers on the back of the hand.

- Hold your hands now as if you were praying. The fingers squeeze tightly. Even tighter.

- As soon as I tell you, please stretch out both index fingers and press them firmly together. Now!

- Now turn your index fingers outwards, both the right and the left.

- Immediately take a look at the space that is created between the fingertips of your index fingers. Imagine having a magnet built into each of your index fingers. Its power would draw your fingertips away from each other and automatically move towards each other again. Here we go!

  To be honest, there are other forces besides the power of suggestion that can make your fingers move towards each other. As soon as the muscles in your hand begin to tire - and they do so after you've clenched your hands for a long time - the index fingers automatically move towards each other. As soon as this first impulse has been perceived by you, you are already convinced that the experiment will work and the fingers, aided by your imagination, move towards each other again. This trick is very well suited to initiate a series of "real" suggestions. We will deal with that later.

A beautiful way into the depths of the self

Before you start the actual hypnosis, you absolutely need the trust of the person whom you want to put into a trance. You have to be sure of that. Imagine if a scruffy guy in ill-fitting eighties clothes and a beer flag suggested that you hypnotize you. I hope you would refuse. By the way, eighty percent of disco and carnival hypnotists look the same, apparently that doesn't bother so many people! Except you of course! So you need your partner's trust, otherwise it won't work. Incidentally, I find it very interesting that there are numerous self-appointed hypnotists who, for example - without any medical training - want to use hypnosis to quit smoking or to slim down and offer their services. It is significant that that many of these life helpers smoke like a chimney and push a decent belly in front of them. Something like that doesn't bother me at all, but it really doesn't fit into the picture they like to draw of themselves. So, watch out and watch out.

Only place yourself in the hands of real experts. I would not trust the offer of such an implausible hypnotist. It is important for you: You create trust when you radiate with every pore that you know exactly what you are doing. And for that you need knowledge and experience. There must be no doubt about your competence. My hypnosis teacher introduced me to the audience on my first attempt with the words: "Here comes a very experienced and well-known hypnotist." That was completely a lie, because I was neither experienced nor known at the time. But with these attributes he did something very important for me, because there was no longer any doubt in the audience that someone is performing here who knows something about his craft. This is a truism: first you need to pick up your partner, before you can take it anywhere. What I mean by that is that very rarely will you meet a person who will instantly fall into a trance just because you imploringly say to them: "Sleep!"

The NLP technique - neurolinguistic programming - which you have already got to know, gives us a very good method of opening up your counterpart to the trance. With the so-called pacing, ie the «matching» or «going along», a consonance is created. So instead of telling you, "You have to yawn now," I should say, "By just sitting and looking at the book, you focus more and more on those words. The more of these words you read and the more you try not to think about them, the more you will feel the irrepressible urge to yawn. " (As I was typing these lines once, I yawned three times.)

The second section is so much more effective because I have already been able to use the situation you are in as a starting point for my suggestion. To get your counterpart in the mood for hypnosis, say something like the following: «Please sit down comfortably. As you sit now, you close your eyes and listen carefully to my words. You can feel the chair under you and your arms on the back of the chair. As you feel all of this and listen to me, you relax deeper and deeper. Your breath is even and calm. You relax deeper and deeper with every word - deeper and deeper. "

This example shows: The art lies in first aligning with pacing and then accommodating two hidden commands for guidance. Your exercise partner will feel his arms on the back of the chair and the chair under his body as soon as you point this out to him. If you initiate the relaxation now, your medium will immediately accept your plan and most likely will react positively to the introduction and follow you. You can also sit down with your medium and have your medium look up at your outstretched index finger. You could say the following sentences: «While you hear my voice and look up at the tip of my index finger, you sit more and more relaxed in your chair. You can feel your eyelids get heavy while listening to me. So it is good. You continue to feel how they blink, and as you listen to me you relax deeper and deeper and feel your eyelids grow heavier and heavier. As you relax deeper and deeper, your eyelids get heavier and heavier. You blink more and more often, and finally your eyes are so tired that they close and you relax deeper and deeper. "

These few lines are tough because they reflect what your counterpart will soon feel. The effect is that everyone gets tired if they look up for a long time and fixate on an object. If you want to increase the show effect, you can use a pendulum or a clock instead of your finger. Don't worry: your eyes will always be heavy on their own. In this situation everyone blinks more and more. So you should watch your partner closely and tell him exactly what you are already observing. So your medium will think, "Wow, my eyes are getting really heavier and I really have to blink more often. Everything the great master says occurs. I sit relaxed on the chair, my eyes become heavier, I blink more and more. " Up to this point everything was still pacing. Leading only comes into play when you are asked to relax. With that he is putting himself more and more in your hands.

Something like real magic works to an outsider: A powerful man has made his medium fall asleep within a few moments. In reality, however, you are only using all the signals you receive from your partner in order to give him feedback with a while-then formula after you have only described what you have observed in him. This is the stuff dreams are made of.

You can also record everything that happens in the auditorium and pass it on to the hypnotized person as feedback. During a show in Hamburg, for example, I asked a lady on stage who was very suggestible, i.e.

responded very strongly to my suggestions. In the course of the introduction (induction) the fan of the air conditioning went on in the theater. Such a thing can tear a test person out of his relaxation immediately and make the hypnosis very difficult or even impossible at that moment. The risk of that happening at that moment was great. The best option seemed to me to be to integrate the noise into the induction. So: «You hear that the ventilation has just started. It sounds a little like the sound of the ocean. The more you pay attention to this sound of the sea, the more you relax ...

Stress

You should always speak your sentences evenly and calmly during the introduction or induction. Imagine Eddie Murphy's voice actor trying to get you into a state of total relaxation. It doesn't really work. The voice of the actor Christian Brückner, for example, who lends his voice to Robert De Niro, has a completely different effect. He could even read the phone book and you would still be listening intently. Only when you appear completely relaxed will your partner follow you. Imagine telling a child something lovingly. This helps.

Let pictures emerge.

Use your words to appeal to all your partner's senses. Create a smooth transition into a state of pleasant consonance by gently pretending what he can see, hear, feel, smell, and also taste. This is how you gently lead him into a trance. By the way: From now on I will consciously use the word "trance" again and again. For us, trance should be the "state of relaxed attention". At this point I will exclude the discussion about whether this state of affairs really exists and where its limits are. This is now counterproductive and has already been done extensively elsewhere.

Suppose you lead your partner in hypnosis after the relaxation phase in his dreams to an orchard under an apple tree. Do not only let the other person see this garden, but also tell them, for example, that it is under the apple tree and that they can feel the grass under their body, smell the scent of the flowers and hear the wind blowing gently through the treetops. Only when all the senses are addressed does the scene feel real to the person concerned and is within their reach. He can then really empathize with the situation. My very good trainer friend, Dr. Ingolf Glabbatz, who will be mentioned more often later, always said the following sentence in his seminars: "He who appeals to all the senses presents the most sensible way."

Make sure, however, that you leave your medium enough space to fill in the gaps in detail that you have planned. For example, they only say that it smells of flowers, but not of which. Your counterpart's orchard will certainly look different from yours. So be careful not to pretend anything that would contradict his view of the situation. The power of images is not to be underestimated. Both the inner images and what we specifically see with our eyes have an incredible impact on how we think. This gives orientation for our behavior and shapes our view of things.

We do what we see

During my lectures and seminars, I often present the following experiment: I ask my audience: "Please raise your hand above your head - just like me", while I myself raise my right hand above my head. After the audience has done this, I look at my watch and continue: "As soon as I say 'now', please go back down with your hand. 3 - 2 - 1 , then I go down with my hand. Almost everyone in the audience followed me straight away and now do the same. After almost all of my hands are down, I say out loud: "Now!"

That's the power of non-verbal communication live. We do what we see rather than what we hear. That means: a picture is worth a thousand words. If you want something from someone, you have to pretend, not pretend. Do you want your children to be on time? Then you should be on time yourself. If you want your employees to be reliable, then you have to be reliable yourself. Simple but true.

You can use your non-verbal statements such as subtext, facial expressions and gestures to show your fellow human beings how you feel and have them read between the lines. Since we almost always use these non-verbal signals unconsciously, we often tend not to take them too seriously. This is a mistake. As we have already seen and will see in the future, the unconscious, the subconscious, is always involved in the communication process. Misunderstandings are not infrequently produced here and must also be clarified here, at this level.

With the correct understanding of details and the knowledge of what to look out for, you can see very well what your counterpart really looks like. A skill that I constantly use on stage to the amazement of my audience. You don't necessarily have to be in the spotlight to use this method successfully.

Let's say you need a new DVD player - I almost wrote a VCR, I'm getting old. First of all, of course, you should know that in the electronics store, the devices that are to be sold most often are always at eye level on the shelf. Heard already? The American says: "Eye level is buy level." Of course: we sell at eye level. It is at this level that things that are second from the left or second from the right in a row are most often grasped. If a salesperson should advertise one of these goods a little too forcefully during the sales pitch, simply ask him: "Would you buy this product?" At that moment you look straight into his eyes. Are the pupils getting bigger, or does he look away for a moment? And then looks at you again? Then you hit the nerve.

The architecture of trance

If you want to try hypnosis yourself, you should think of the process like guided relaxation instructions, which are introduced by suggestion formulas. Some people will get involved in something like this very quickly and without reservation, others will fight back downright against it, because such a rest makes them afraid of losing control! How much someone responds to your suggestions - it is also said how "suggestible" someone is - can depend on many factors, for example whether they consider you to be trustworthy, whether they have a strong imagination, or whether they indulge well without reservation can. You should break your hypnosis down into five separate steps:

1. *To prepare:*Explain to your medium what you are up to and you will feel whether they have confidence in you. Now you can initiate the first light trance - as described above.

2. *Deepening:* Deepen it by asking your partner to go down an elevator and come back, for example.

3. *Testing:*Is your partner really in the state you want? You can check this by observing that he is really doing everything exactly as you tell him to.

4. *To lead:* Make your suggestions calmly and watch your medium closely.

5. *Wake:* Bring your partner back to real time.

The suggestions you convey depend on your goal. A therapist will certainly want to suggest different things than a hypnotist in a discotheque who makes his test subjects think they are Elvis Presley and expects a corresponding show. During hypnosis on stage, one sees again and again that the hypnotist gives the medium commands that are only to be carried out after the subject is conscious again. And that works. For this reason, it is imperative that at the end of each session you make sure that all suggestions are cleared!

To prepare

Provide silence. If you want, you can have quiet music playing in the background, but this is not absolutely necessary. I myself can't stand the pan flute tooting in the spa areas of many hotels any more than the background annoyance from the tooting in our Chinese restaurant. Almost as bad as some radio stations with more advertisements than anything else.

In any case, make sure that you are undisturbed. And make yourself aware that you are not creating a situation that the other person would not already know, you are just pretending to do so. You work exclusively with the expectations of your partner, which also means that he would never do anything that he does not do while awake. However, if you seem insecure, the chances are bad that the other person will respond to your suggestions. You have to be self-confident and convincing and, even on the first try, give the impression that you've done the whole thing very often.

As soon as your partner is sitting calmly and relaxed in the chair, you could, for example, have them tense all the muscles in the body at the same time. The breath continues to flow calmly, but all muscles - starting with the feet, through the legs, stomach, chest, shoulders and arms to the fingertips - should be contracted at the same time. After a few moments, the tension should be released again.

Now you can pace and load knowing that the body will feel heavier after this pass. They speak the following formula: As your body gets heavier and heavier, your breathing becomes more and more even and calm. You breathe calmly, are relaxed and hear my voice. You sink deeper and deeper into your chair and just let my words carry you away. "

Deepen

In reality, there is no real trance that you can deepen. However, the image of sliding deeper into a state of relaxation is very strong and therefore very easy for your partner to visualize. So once you notice that he is sagging a little and his muscles are loosening, you can take that state further. I really enjoy doing this by letting my medium visualize an elevator that slowly slides down floor by floor. Emphasize that each time he reaches the next floor he will relax more and more.

At this point I should clear up some misconceptions about hypnosis. It is possible that the other person has higher expectations and thinks that they will fall asleep right away or experience something they have never experienced before. Then it may be that the disappointment is great. With these false expectations, your counterpart could have the impression that what you are doing is not going to work. However, you are dependent on working with the expectations and assumptions of your counterpart. The medium has to be convinced on the one hand that it will slide into a trance and on the other hand believe that everything will go exactly as planned. In order to be able to ensure this, explain at this point that while the other person relaxes deeper and deeper, they can still understand and hear everything, what you say. It will also always remain fully aware that it is currently in a state of trance. With this sentence you take out false expectations and direct attention where you want it to go.

Now announce that you will now be counting backwards from ten to zero and that your medium will see and feel the elevator descending with each new number in the display. As soon as you arrive in the basement, the elevator has also reached the very bottom in the depths of consciousness. Mention that the other person will then be in a state of pleasant and deep relaxation.

Now let your partner go down in the elevator and pace everything you watch - "As you slide down, while you hear my voice, while you go down one floor, you relax deeper and deeper."

Testing

If you have the impression that your partner is now in the state you want, you can test whether he is actually following your instructions. For example, you can suggest to him that the door will open on the lowest floor and that your test subject will now enter a beautiful garden. Remember to address all of your senses again. Don't get too specific about this. Do not say that there are paths or special pots with Arabic patterns in the garden. If this is important to you, at least let the other person decide where these things are. Emphasize that the garden is beautiful and that the other person can return to it whenever they want. For example, you could ask him to find an apple tree and take a seat under it. An apple is close enough to touch. Please pick this apple with his right hand. That is the order. If the right arm goes up now, everything is okay. If not, then you need to go deeper.

Give suggestions

In the best case scenario, the test described above will not only help you to check whether your counterpart is responding to your suggestions. It will also help you deepen the trance even further. Assuming the arm went up, your partner should now slowly lower the hand with the apple in it. Now comes the deepening: You say that with every little bit with which the arm moves down, your counterpart relaxes deeper and deeper. You can also build in a very effective loop at this point by asking:

"The more the arm moves down, the deeper you relax, and the deeper you relax, the more the arm moves down."

Your counterpart follows you completely. Now continue to use the picture of the garden and the apple tree. In the imagination, the person opposite is already on the chair. He should mentally drop the picked apple in his right hand as soon as the arm is back on the back of the chair. Now you can suggest that the right arm is getting heavier and heavier. So heavy that it sticks firmly to the back of the chair. Have him imagine that an invisible force was tying his arm tightly to the chair. Now may he try to free his arm from this force and lift something. A key term in this formula is the word "try" - that already implies that it will not be possible to raise your arm. Now there are three options. First: the arm goes up.

Second, your partner tries to raise his arm
but it doesn't work. Third: the person
opposite does nothing and sits motionless on
the chair.

For our purposes, the second option is
of course the best. If your counterpart does
not move at all, it can of course be that they
are extremely relaxed and therefore do not
even have the strength to try to comply with
the request. Assuming the arm goes up
despite the suggestions, then hopefully it
will at least feel heavy. In this case, you
work with it and say, "Very well - and while
you feel that your arm has somehow got
heavier, you move it down again, and with
every bit that the arm moves down, you
relax more deeply , and with every bit you
let go more and more. " You simply record
every feedback from your counterpart and
link it to a suggestion.

Assuming that the suggestion worked, you can now go a step further and make your arm lighter: "A helium balloon is now hanging on your right arm, pulling it upwards. Your arm is getting lighter and lighter. The balloon pulls him up, on and on. " Pay attention to your partner's right arm, as soon as the hand twitches or moves slightly upwards, pick up this signal and immediately say: "Very good, your arm moves upwards, on and on." At some point the arm will slowly move upwards.

It may take a while for this movement to come. Please note: With this suggestion it is very important that you constantly take in every feedback and extremely pace it. As soon as the hand is all the way up, you can suggest to your partner that he should gently lower it back down. Here you should use the downward movement of the arm to deepen the trance: "The deeper the arm sinks, the deeper you come into the state of absolute relaxation, and the deeper you relax, the lower your arm sinks."

The imaginary garden is a beautiful idea. It's a lovely place that your partner can retreat to anytime once they invent it. Such a mental retreat can be very valuable. It is a very personal space that you can dream of at any time when you feel stress, are afraid or just want to have some peace and quiet to escape from everyday life. In the rare cases in which I do not fall asleep immediately at night, I either play the guitar in my head and practice scales that are not yet one hundred percent, or withdraw to my very own dream oasis. There I can design everything according to my wishes and do what I want. In the process, I inevitably relax so deeply that I can fall asleep in no time if I intend to.

So you can do your practice partner a big favor by telling him that he can return to this dream location at any time if he feels the need to. This can arise before an important exam or before a moment when he needs your full attention. He should then always simply imagine the elevator mentioned at the beginning. Take the elevator down and suddenly step into his dream garden. In any case, explain to him that if he goes on his dream journey alone, he can open his eyes at any time and come back from his trance. Whenever he wanted to. This can arise before an important exam or before a moment when he needs your full attention. He should then always simply imagine the elevator mentioned at the beginning. Take the elevator down and suddenly step into his dream garden. In any case, explain to him that if he goes on his dream journey alone, he can open his eyes at any time and come back from his trance. Whenever he wanted to. This can arise before an important exam or before a moment when he needs your full attention. He should then always simply imagine the elevator mentioned at the beginning. Take the elevator down and suddenly step into his dream garden. In any case, explain to him that if he goes on his dream journey alone, he can open his eyes at any time and come back from his trance. Whenever he wanted to.

Wake

At the end of the session it is very important to gently lead the partner back into the here and now, to wake him up again. To do this, let him get back into the elevator, which is now going straight up. I myself count from zero to ten out loud while I'm driving. Tell him that with each floor the heaviness disappears from his body and that more and more energy will return to his body. Once you get to ten, ask your partner to open their eyes again and breathe deeply in and out again. With each number, your voice is getting firmer again, becoming more and more like the way you normally use it in conversation. Well, of course it depends on how you normally talk to people around you - but I think you get what I mean.

After your partner is fully in the here and now again, you can ask questions to test their effects. If you want, you could ask how real the garden felt, sounded, and how real it looked. The questions about the duration of the exercises are always astonishing. Good test subjects often think that the session was much shorter than it actually was. Often half an hour feels like a minute. Let your partner know that he can put himself into a trance with this exact method from now on, if he only practices it correctly.

Once you've mastered the technique outlined above, you could go a step further and try a post hypnotic command. To do this, of course, you need a partner who responds well to your suggestions. Not everyone who has had the arm gluing and raising will respond to a post-hypnotic command. Nevertheless, the chances are good that it will work if everything else has worked smoothly so far. So after you have sent your counterpart to the dream garden and the arm tests all work, you can give the first post-hypnotic command: "Every time I touch your forehead and say the word 'sleep' you are immediately back in this state pleasant relaxation, each time deeper than before. Every time I snap my fingers next to your ear are you wide awake and feeling fresh. " Now very important: "If you have understood everything I said, please nod your head." This feedback shows you that your counterpart really clearly perceived what needs to be done. Now snap your fingers. Your counterpart should "wake up". Wait a moment and make sure that she is really awake. Then look him in the eye, touch his forehead, and then say again: "Sleep." If it drifts away now, you have full control - and with it a huge responsibility! what to do. Now snap your fingers. Your counterpart should "wake up". Wait a moment and make sure that she is really awake. Then look him in the eye, touch his forehead, and then say again: "Sleep." If it drifts away now, you have full control - and with it a huge responsibility! what to do. Now snap your fingers. Your counterpart should "wake up". Wait a moment and make sure that she is really awake. Then look him in the eye, touch his forehead, and then say again: "Sleep." If it drifts away now, you have full control - and with it a huge responsibility!

If you've come this far, the next step could be trying to get your partner to forget their name. The best way to do this is to say: "If you wake up right away, you won't be able to remember your name. The more you try, the more you will forget about him. It's on the tip of your tongue but you just can't remember it, and the harder you try to find it, the less it will occur to you. Just as you can sometimes no longer remember the name of someone you know, you can no longer remember your name. When I ask your name, you can't remember him. The more you try, the more it will be forgotten. If you open your eyes right away, you will have forgotten him. "

Now snap your fingers. Look your counterpart in the eye and ask for their name again. In doing so, set the undertone as if you didn't expect it to give you the right answer. Shake your head slightly at the question to indicate that it is unlikely to work. If it can tell you its name anyway, don't worry. Just try it later - even with a wide variety of people. No master has fallen from the sky yet.

Just as you gave posthypnotic commands before, you could delete them. All you have to do is tell your partner that all the suggestions you gave him are now completely erased. You only exist in the consciousness of your counterpart. It works best if you lead him back into his trance with the word "sleep" and the touch on his forehead and then tell him that all suggestions have been lifted again. Explain to the other person that they will be wide awake and fully recovered and that they will no longer be under hypnosis as soon as they have opened their eyes. From then on, all suggestions are canceled and it will immediately be able to remember its name again.

That was it, the short, brief introduction to the big world of hypnosis. Please note that you carry out all experiments at your own risk. In itself, I have only described these methods in detail to show you how a trance is basically structured and how it can be brought about in the medium. I didn't write these lines to guide cocky thugs on how to put others into a trance at parties or in the schoolyard. Because that is not to be trifled with. Particularly when it comes to suggestions, one should exercise the utmost caution and, above all, turn on one's mind before attempting to penetrate someone else's.

Responsibility is the term that fits exactly at this point. If you yourself are not in control of your senses, you should quickly get away from the psyche of others. This is best illustrated by the following story: A (very stupid!) Hypnotist has a very suggestible audience on stage. He gives it numerous post-hypnotic commands. Among other things, he suggests to him that he - the hypnotist - will from now on be invisible to the viewer. It works. The hypnotist moves some objects back and forth on the stage and the audience thinks they are flying. Then he puts the viewer back into a trance and says: "Now you can no longer see or hear me." Some people's stupidity really knows no bounds. How is he supposed to get his audience out of the trance, when he can no longer hear him? We don't know how the story ended up in the end.

Notepad for aspiring hypnotists

If you really want to hypnotize someone - and you have realized that you can handle it responsibly - there are a few points that you should be aware of:

- Never hypnotize a person with psychological difficulties or even severe ailments, such as epilepsy. If you have any doubts about someone's mental health, stay away from it.

- Don't play the hobby therapist. You must leave all medical and therapeutic measures to the specialist. In no case should you experiment with this.

- Hypnosis is a gentle method. Avoid show effects and make sure that the test subjects feel comfortable with you. Then you have the best chance to see what a great instrument you have mastered. A tool that you can use to calm yourself and others down. A tool that can ensure that others are doing well.

- Once the trance is reached, everything contributes to the hypnosis. This means that you always have to make sure in advance that everything can go as planned. Clarify all eventualities. Ask your medium if they have any allergies. Because even an imaginary bite into an apple or lemon can have far-reaching consequences. Each of your words should be chosen with great care. A hypnotist once said to his viewer: "You are now sitting on a great motorcycle, a really hot stove." Whereupon the viewer jumped up screaming and got blisters on his legs - like a real burn.

- In the end, make sure that your subject is free from any suggestions you have given them and that they also know that they are no longer hypnotized. Think of the hypnotist in the amusement park, luckily he was still available.

- It is best to see hypnosis as an instrument to help others calm down and relax, as a kind of mental oasis. As I said, you'd better leave the rest to the professionals.

Dangers of hypnosis

A popular myth has it that a hypnotized person cannot be ordered to commit crimes. Any command that contradicts the values and ethical standards of the hypnotized person would immediately wake the person out of the trance. In my opinion this is complete nonsense. An experienced hypnotist can loosely bypass internal blockages and defenses in the medium.

I myself was a witness when a very competent hypnotist put a gun into the hand of a subject and then explained to him that he was on a safari. A real lion stands in front of him and he - the hypnotized - can only survive and repel the lion's attack if he shoots at him. If he didn't, the lion would attack him and eat him skin and hair. In reality, a man, not a lion, was standing in front of the hypnotized person. At the command of the hypnotist, the medium fired at him from the alarm pistol until he was brought out of the trance again: It is very possible to get hypnotized people to commit crimes. If you - as described above - choose detours and use a clever trick. Hopefully the viewer would not have heard the command «Shoot the person in front of you». But even that cannot be ruled out with absolute certainty. After the audience woke up from the trance, they had been told what had just happened. He was shocked.

The question of whether or not crimes can be committed under hypnosis has long preoccupied some researchers. In order to get on the track, some of them not only risked their careers, but also put their health on the line. I found a very interesting article on this topic in 2009 in the Neue Zürcher Zeitung. Numerous astonishing attempts in this field have been described here.

One of the most famous hypnosis researchers is Harcourt Stebbins. For example, he wanted to know if a student would throw a glass of nitric acid on his face under hypnosis. The experimental set-up was actually simple, and of course the glass of acid would be swapped for another glass of water at the right moment without being noticed. But people make mistakes - and in this experiment the person in charge simply forgot to change the glass after several attempts. So the student poured acid on his professor's face. Thanks to the quick help from doctors at home, he only left a small scar on his scalp. Blessing in disguise! That happened in 1942 at Louisiana State University in Baton Rouge.

The aforementioned doctor Ambroise-Auguste Liébault wrote about hypnosis: "The sleeper is transformed into an automaton that can be shaped and manipulated as the mood takes you." That is exactly what still fascinates people today about this phenomenon. You can tell someone something, they do it, and later they can't remember what they did.

Even today it is debated whether this is true or not for all kinds of commands. In my very personal opinion, this argument is idle. As always, there is no clear yes or no answer to the question. The two examples given above already show that blind obedience works in many cases. And there are sure to be cases when it didn't work. In my opinion, this is exactly where the answer can be found: It works for some and it doesn't work for others. And that's enough to exercise great caution. Because there is still the danger that something can happen. And there is nothing to gloss over it.

As early as 1884, experiments were made to show whether a test person would poison someone close to them with arsenic or not and another would shoot someone on command. In fact, neither of them hesitated and carried out the act, but nothing happened. Of course the pistol wasn't loaded, and the arsenic wasn't arsenic either, just powdered sugar. The experiment was carried out and published by Jules Liégeois. By the way: Not only was murder carried out under hypnosis, promissory notes have also been forged!

Despite the clear results of Liégeois' experiments, more and more critics came on the scene: The experiments were purely laboratory tests and the test subjects knew that they were not actually loaded weapons or real poison. So Liégeois publicly demonstrated his experiment in front of professors and politicians with a woman who, on command, stabbed wildly with a knife and shot a pistol. The invited panel of critics left the room in shock. Nice detail: Numerous students remained in the room. They ordered the hypnotized young lady to undress immediately. However, she refused to accept this order.

Incidentally, the same experiment was reproduced again fifty years later at the University of California. Here the test subject began to undress so quickly that the professor was just able to stop her before it became really embarrassing. No wonder! It was later found out that she was a part-time stripper.

Lloyd W. Rowland from the University of Tulsa in Oklahoma also did research in the field of hypnosis. His test subjects also poured acid over the experimenter in a trance. This time, however, against a pane of glass, invisible to her, behind which the hypnotist was. Then Rowland wanted to know if the hypnotized would harm themselves not only to others. To do this, he pissed a rattlesnake until it became extremely aggressive, and then put it in a box that was open to the front. He informed the hypnotized test participants that there was a rubber rope in the box and asked them to take the contents out at his command. According to Rowland, the snake in the box had already raised its head and rattled so loudly that it could be heard thirty yards away.

Three out of four participants put into the box. Fortunately there was a pane of glass here too and nothing happened to anyone. In addition to the hypnotized test subjects, there were also forty-two non-hypnotized control groups. Not a single one of them obeyed orders. Most of them didn't even approach the box.

This study showed that the widespread belief that a hypnotized person does nothing that violates their moral code is unsustainable. The original study was carried out as early as the 1930s, but the misconception persists. In the 1940s, the acid experiment described above was carried out in Louisiana. That was stupid for Harcourt Stebbins without safety glass. But even after that it didn't seem to be enough evidence to convince people otherwise.

In the course of these studies, further experiments were carried out with snakes. A medium passed out immediately after being bitten. The animals were non-poisonous diamond water snakes. In this attempt, seven out of eight people had carried out the commands under hypnosis. This means to take notes: In "immoral" hands, hypnosis can very well become a very dangerous instrument for the abolition of free will.

The four realities

The real journey of discovery does not consist in exploring new landscapes, but in seeing them with new eyes, Marcel Proust recognizes that very correctly. And so the psychologist Serge King makes the suggestion in one of his seminars to simply assume that there is not just one reality, but four of them. In reality, of course, there are as many conceptions of reality as there are people. But my aim here is just to show that you can take multiple perspectives. Already the division into four ways of looking at the world has the great advantage that you always have the opportunity to change your perspective if you are stuck on your level. However, my aim is not to evaluate the respective perspectives, they are all equally good or bad.

1. objective reality,

2. subjective reality,

3. symbolic reality,

4. holistic reality.

Objectively and really

This view is closest to our western thinking. The characteristic: You look at things separately from one another. Say: I am me and you are you. Mine is mine and yours is yours. It is also extremely useful and appropriate in many areas of life. This is how things can be divided into groups. I think that is precisely why the majority of scientists look at the world this way. If one has the scientific principles of thought in mind, the objectified worldview certainly also leads to the "correct" path to knowledge. Distinguishing between different aspects and drawing attention to the differences can in many cases be useful for knowledge.

An example: If your team has won a competition, it is nice for you to somehow belong to the group of winners and celebrate together with the champions. Or: I am very grateful when my pharmacist gives me exactly the medicine that is right for me at the moment, i.e. when he differentiates between this one and all the others that he still has in the store. Paying too much attention to differences can also be destructive. For example, those who focus too much on the differences between people will soon have a greater tendency towards fear or xenophobia. As always, it depends on the right moment and the optimal dose.

The subjective reality

With that, the world looks a little different. You may be very fond of someone who some of your friends don't like. At the level of subjective reality, you just like him. I hope that I will be spared the fact that my daughter's choice of her first boyfriend has a different subjective reality than my wife and I! That means: Everything that you subjectively belongs to this area. Millions of people enjoy watching "Musikantenstadl" and listening to pop music. According to the subjective reality of this group, this type of entertainment is comfortable for them. I - in my subjective reality - cannot share this view and I stand for Stevie Ray Vaughan. Many other people feel the same way in terms of taste. But who is right now? Nobody and everyone. Whether I'm right or not depends on which group I feel entertained by, the guitar freaks or the musicians. The only criterion by which we judge the authenticity of something is via the question of whether another person has also experienced something or not. Even that is sometimes not enough - if something does not suit us (even as a group), then we can still dismiss the others as weirdos or dreamers and thus maintain our subjective point of view.

At the level of subjective reality, it is always about our relationship with the world. Our experience is determined by our belief, that's what we assume. Because the world is what we think it is. Our thinking has a decisive influence on our perception. For example: A decision does not directly change what will happen in the future. Rather, after you have made the decision, your thinking influences what happens - entirely subjectively.

The symbolic reality

This is the reality we perceive when we dream. This not only means the dreams of the night, but also our daydreams, as well as the goals that we set for ourselves. At the level of language, metaphors fall into this category. If something is not going as you imagine it should, it can make a lot of sense to switch from the subjective or objective point of view to the symbolic one. Some scientists have successfully made use of this technique. Sir Isaac Newton allegedly dropped an apple on his head one day and - heureka - he then established the law of gravity. The chemist Friedrich August Kekulé von Stradonitz deciphered the structure of benzene in a dream. He reported that he had dreamed of carbon and hydrogen atoms dancing. He also dreamed of a snake that bit its tail. Only through this dream did he find the solution to his problem. And it all moved on a symbolic level.

During my school days we often played a game that was about guessing which classmate someone was thinking about. We then asked questions like, "If the person you are thinking of were a car, what kind of car would they be?" Or: "Which drink would you be?" After a few questions someone always found out which classmate was meant. Incidentally, I still feel sorry for my classmate on tractor chamomile tea and lentil stew. But what the heck, today he's a dentist ...

Games like these can be great fun and there is a lot to learn from symbols. It is interesting to see how others think of you and also to see how I think of others. I know a beautiful mind game that takes place on the symbolic level.

Symbol game

* Have your guests pick up any object from the room while having a nice dinner.

* Now have them use this to describe themselves. I will show you how the book you are holding right now and I will describe myself about this work.

* «The book is narrow, like me too. It is multi-faceted and makes you laugh in some places and thought-provoking in others. There are a lot of crazy thoughts and ideas in this book. The book has some secrets - a few reveals it, a few keeps it to themselves ... »

I could go on like this for a very long time to explain myself using this book, i.e. a symbol. Remember: The term "mental training" has often appeared elsewhere. Among other things, it is about putting yourself in a comfortable state of being and dreaming in a targeted manner. Depending on the needs, these dreams are designed in a way that makes sense for our thinking. This, too, is nothing more than a change into symbolic reality, which we can conveniently shape according to our wishes. This is used in many areas of life. By the way: If you as a sprinter try to remember past victories at the starting position in order to consciously put yourself in good shape, then that is not helpful. It has been proven that we move back as soon as we think of past events and immediately a little forward as soon as we think of the future. For this reason, it is important to imagine at the start how you will be on the podium. As a result, we automatically move forward better, which seems to be desirable during a sprint.

The holistic reality

There are no limits, that is the principle of holistic reality. This perspective is in stark contrast to the objective perspective. At first sight, this assumption seems to us to be nonsensical. After all, we are constantly reaching our limits. Because we can only hear within a few hundred meters, for example. Our lives are limited, as are the earth's resources as a whole and our bank account in particular. From an objective point of view, these statements are all true. That's exactly what it's all about - to see things by putting on new glasses that were previously hidden from us. After all, the world is what we think it is. So let's just change our perspective here, and let's not think within narrow limits. Study the starry sky at night, the distances you can guess, are infinite: there are apparently no limits, everything is one. In our minds we can actually remove all of these limits. For example the one between two people. If your child has done a great job and you are proud of it, then this is a moment when the boundary between you and your child dissolves. If your partner is sad and you are also sad for this reason alone, then look at the world from a holistic corner at that moment. If you suffer and cheer for a film with the hero, likewise. Such behavior cannot take place on the objective level. After all, the person in the film is not real. She's not really near you yet. For example the one between two people. If your child has done a great job and you are proud of it, then this is a moment when the boundary between you and your child dissolves. If your partner is sad and you are also sad for this reason alone, then look at the world from a holistic corner at that moment. If you suffer and cheer for a film with the hero, likewise. Such behavior cannot take place on the objective level. After all, the person in the film is not real. She's not really near you yet. For example the one between two people. If your child has done a great job and you are proud of it, then this is a moment when the boundary between you and your child dissolves. If your partner is sad and you are also sad for this reason alone, then look at the world from a holistic corner at that moment. If you suffer and cheer for a film with the hero, likewise. Such behavior cannot take place on the objective level. After all, the person in the film is not real. She's not really near you yet. then look at the world in the moment from the holistic corner. If you suffer and cheer for a film with the hero, likewise. Such behavior cannot take place on the objective level. After all, the person in the film is not real. She's not really near you yet. then look at the world in the moment from the holistic corner. If you suffer and cheer for a film with the hero, likewise. Such behavior cannot take place on the objective level. After all, the person in the film is not real. She's not really near you yet.

We can also be connected to objects. Let's say you've been saving for your car for a long time. Proudly park it within sight and have a coffee. From a distance, you can see someone leaning against your car. In that moment, you'll feel like that person is getting too close to you - and not your car. In that moment you are in the holistic reality. The same is true when a dance couple virtually merges in motion and thus forms a unity. Just as rider and horse become one.

In our world of thoughts there will only ever be those limitations that we allow. "Think what you want" is therefore more than just an invitation, it is a concrete possibility. In our minds we can do everything we can think and be everything. Within seconds we can dream of every place on earth and in space that magically attracts us. If I ever have a bad day, I dream of New York, the Maldives or the South of France - depending on where I want to go most at the moment. Of course, through the objective glasses I am not there - through the symbolic and holistic glasses I am. If it now becomes clear to us that consciousness does not differentiate between experiences that we have actually experienced and those that we only imagine pictorially enough,

As an author, speaker and artist, I constantly change these levels and deal with the world in a playful way. You could do the same thing to see everything around you with different eyes. Most of the time you cannot change the world, but you can change your view of things.

Influencing methods with real impact

The following experiment shows how unnoticed influencing can actually work. I found it in Ian Harling's and Martin Nyrup's book Sleight of Mind. It's really worth trying the experiment the two of them describe.

Activate the olfactory anchor

You don't need a lot for this: five playing cards, a spectator and a little bit of perfume. To prepare, all you have to do is put a little scented water on one of the cards. Let's say the scented card is the ace of spades. The values of the other playing cards are indifferent. The card should only smell a little bit if you hold it very close to your face.

The scent trail

- Now you need a teammate. Place the five playing cards in a row in front of him. The sides of the cards should face the table, the backs facing up. So your fellow player only sees the back of the cards.

- Now ask your teammate to close their eyes and breathe calmly. Slowly tell him that his other senses are now particularly sharpened because he can keep his eyes closed and concentrate fully on the experiment. Now, in order to increase your chances of success, you need to call his attention to the sense of smell without addressing it explicitly. You can do this easily by asking him to focus on his breathing.

- Let your teammate breathe deeply and calmly. While breathing in, he should concentrate on his stomach in this experiment. If you have the impression that your teammate is relaxed and breathing regularly, you can continue. Tell him to keep his eyes closed while you explain to others what is about to happen. Turn over all the cards on the table to prove that they are all different.

- Turn all cards over again except for the ace of spades. Take the said card in your hand and hold it in front of your opponent's forehead. Tell him that you are now thinking about the card. You do too! But it is important that you hold the card in front of his forehead in such a way that he unconsciously perceives the scent. To encourage him, supportively tell him to focus on all of his senses while you hold the card in front of his forehead. May he pay attention to everything he hears and feels - including his shallow and regular breathing!

He should open himself to all impressions and simply feel how the card feels.

- Now put the card back in its place. So now there is a row of playing cards on the table, all of them face up.

- Now your teammate should open his eyes again. Show him the five cards on the table and explain to him that he should now take one card at a time and hold it to his forehead. If he wants, he can close his eyes again. Advise him not to say anything or commit himself to a card until he has held all the cards to his forehead.

- When he is done with it, he should intuitively point to the map that, in his opinion, was previously held on his forehead. His decision really has to be made without thinking!

You will be amazed at your own magic. The number works astonishingly often. Since the scent is only perceived very subtly, your teammate does not know himself why he has chosen the right card. Incidentally, you will further increase your chances if you place the perfumed card in the second position from the right. Conversely: If your teammate is left-handed, place the card in the second position from the left.

Instruments of influence

In addition to hypnosis and suggestion, there are of course numerous other methods of influencing. Usually they work without a trance induction. For me, the psychologist Robert B. Cialdini - that's really his name, it's not an artist name - is one of the best researchers in this field. In my opinion, his book "The Psychology of Persuasion" is groundbreaking. Here Robert B. Cialdini deals exclusively with the factors that lead to one person doing something that another would like. He investigates which techniques there are to suggest something to another person and to make him compliant.

After all his research, he finally comes to the conclusion that there are thousands of techniques - many of which I will introduce you to here - but almost all of which fall into six categories. Each of these six contains a psychological principle, which in turn has a decisive influence on our behavior. These are:

- Reciprocity,

- Consistency,

- social reliability,

- Sympathy,

- Authority and

- Scarcity.

There is no way I want to go into the dark side of power with this book and what I write here. So I am not describing these methods so that you can use them, but solely so that you can learn about them. You would of course be able to do so after reading this book, but you should just leave it. My only intention is to make these methods transparent for you, and I want you to be able to draw insights from them. From now on you will recognize manipulators and you will no longer get pissed off! Unmask the secrets that may have remained hidden from you before. You will learn how manipulators use these instruments as soon as they want to talk you into something, be it to purchase a product, to make a donation or to make a concession on your part. It looks as if knowledge about it is becoming more and more important, because in our fast-moving times with an ever-increasing flood of information that crashes on us around the clock because we are always available, we are obviously at risk of manipulation more and more often. Transparency and awareness of the dangers is a good form of defense that can be used successfully.

You should be clear about one thing: We humans have usually internalized certain stimulus-response mechanisms that we often cannot get out of. Especially when we are under pressure or stress, we resort to behaviors that have already served us well in the past. That is neither good nor bad. It just turned out to be useful in the course of evolution. Due to our type of selection, we can usually separate the important from the unimportant and get through everyday life without much thought. Typical stimulus-response mechanisms make life easier for us under normal circumstances.

Incidentally, I believe that coffee house chains like "Starbucks" only have the "Coffee of the day" for this reason. It was invented for people like me. The incredible offer on the board regularly overwhelms me. But since I don't want to be seen as a predictable boring person in front of my wife who always orders the same thing, I have a trick: I keep ordering this "Coffee of the day". In this way I can bring a nice variation into the order and still don't have to spend too much energy thinking about which of the 25,000 types of coffee I should order. My behavior in this case is just practical and works automatically. The world is already complicated enough, so in this case I like to take the opportunity to

So under normal circumstances it helps us a lot to have a pattern of behavior available that makes our life easier. We have such prejudices for a reason. Under normal circumstances, they make a comfortable life possible for us: They help us to be a little light. Usually, no insidious person comes to us and shamelessly exploits these mechanisms for his harmful ambitions.

Please read the following numerals and at the end state the next number:

one thousand ninety-four,

one thousand ninety-five,

one thousand ninety-six,

one thousand ninety-seven,

one thousand ninety-eight,

one thousand ninety-nine.

Please complete the next number.

Did you also name the two thousand? Then you acted like almost everyone with whom I have already carried out this test. Even so, the answer remains wrong. The correct number is, of course, one thousand one hundred. Robert B. Cialdini calls this mechanism "click-surr behavior". It's made up of behaviors that are practically the same every time. They are repeatedly caused by certain triggers. I'll give you another example.

Alphabet twist experiment

Please read the following word loud and clear: Window sills. That wasn't loud enough, so please again: window sills. Now a twist of the letter: Bensterfänke. That was still a little indistinct, please again: Bensterfänke. So, now please say the following word out loud: Dizzy.

Ain't that a thing With only very minor modifications, we can be influenced in such a way that we emphasize a word incorrectly because we immediately orientate ourselves on another word. If such behavior can be triggered within so few turns of phrase, how much do you think our fellow human beings and our environment can use all possible means to ensure that such patterns are engraved in our consciousness? Just imagine how easy we are to crack for someone who knows what makes us tick!

opposites attract

We have one possibility of using such patterns with the so-called contrast principle of human perception. The underlying principle says that we often perceive two things as different than they actually are when we are confronted with them in direct succession. So let's say you drive your car one hundred and ninety kilometers per hour on the freeway. If you brake now, take the next exit and turn into a town, the fifty kilometers per hour that you now have to drive will seem very slow to you. But as soon as you leave a 30 km / h zone and accelerate to fifty kilometers per hour, you feel like Sebastian Vettel. This is what you mean by the contrast principle.

A very notable example is given by Robert B. Cialdini in relation to how much attractiveness we attach to a fellow human being. For example, if we talk to a very beautiful specimen of the opposite sex and then to a less attractive one, then this second person will appear less attractive to us than he "actually" is. To my female readers, suppose you first talk to Johnny Depp's doppelganger, then every other man suddenly feels like King Kong's shaved brother. To my male readers, thank goodness Depp and Clooney have very few doubles. They also have really stupid last names for us Germans, especially good Johnny.

According to a study by DT Kenrick, SE Gutierres and LL Goldberg from 1989, the beauty craze and the resulting portrayal of very attractive people in the media - in series, films, casting shows - can lead to us becoming less satisfied with the appearance of our current one or future partner. Further studies by these researchers suggest that looking at nude photographs of sexually very attractive people can lead to one's partner becoming less sexually attractive. The world is always what we think it is! I can think of a nice word from Eckart von Hirschhausen about this. In his program «Glücksbringer» he said: «The people in the newspapers don't look like the people in the newspapers either. "This certainty alone should remind us again and again. Nowadays you can no longer believe the pictures in magazines and films. There is a very good trick so that you no longer allow yourself to be manipulated by the fashion industry: Look for pictures on the Internet that show your ideals of beauty in underwear. Furthermore, you should always keep in mind that with so-called retouchers there is an entire branch of work that turns attractive people into absolutely flawlessly beautiful people. The computer world offers wonderful technical possibilities. Only in pictures, mind you, in reality all these oh-so-perfect people have to go to the bathroom first thing in the morning. A visit to the following website can also be very helpful in this regard: Nowadays you can no longer believe the pictures in magazines and films. There is a very good trick so that you no longer allow yourself to be manipulated by the fashion industry: Look for pictures on the Internet that show your ideals of beauty in underwear. Furthermore, you should always keep in mind that with so-called retouches there is an entire branch of work that turns attractive people into absolutely flawlessly beautiful people. The computer world offers wonderful technical possibilities. Only in pictures, mind you, in reality all these oh-so-perfect people have to go to the bathroom first thing in the morning. A visit to the following website can also be very helpful in this regard: Nowadays you can no longer believe the pictures in magazines and films. There is a very good trick so that you no longer allow yourself to be manipulated by the fashion industry: Look for pictures on the Internet that show your ideals of beauty in underwear. Furthermore, you should always keep in mind that with so-called retouchers there is an entire branch of work that turns attractive people into absolutely flawlessly beautiful people. The computer world offers wonderful technical possibilities. Only in pictures, mind you, in reality all these oh-so-perfect people have to go to the bathroom first thing in the morning. A visit to the following website can also be very helpful in this regard: There is a very good trick so that you no longer allow yourself to be manipulated by the fashion industry: Look for pictures on the Internet that show your ideals of beauty in underwear. Furthermore, you should always keep in mind that with so-called retouchers there is an entire branch of work that turns attractive people into absolutely flawlessly beautiful people. The computer world offers wonderful technical possibilities. Only in pictures, mind you, in reality all these oh-so-perfect people have to go to the bathroom first thing in the morning. A visit to the following website can also be very helpful in this regard: There is a very good trick so that you no longer allow yourself to be manipulated by the fashion industry: Look for pictures on the Internet that show your ideals of beauty in underwear. Furthermore, you should always keep in mind that with so-called retouchers there is an entire branch of work that turns attractive people into absolutely flawlessly beautiful people. The computer world offers wonderful technical possibilities. Only in pictures, mind you, in reality all these oh-so-perfect people have to go to the bathroom first thing in the morning. A visit to the following website can also be very helpful in this regard: that with the so-called retouchers there is a whole profession that turns attractive people into absolutely flawlessly beautiful people. The computer world offers wonderful technical possibilities. Only in pictures, mind you, in reality all these oh-so-perfect people have to go to the bathroom first thing in the morning. A visit to the following website can also be very helpful in this regard: that with the so-called retouchers there is a whole profession that turns attractive people into absolutely flawlessly beautiful people. The computer world offers wonderful technical possibilities. Only in pictures, mind you, in reality all these oh-so-perfect people have to go to the bathroom first thing in the morning. A visit to the following website can also be very helpful in this Glenn Feron is a master of the "Art of Retouching", the art of retouching. First look at the models depicted as beautiful beings - and then look at them before the master has edited the pictures. This can be very healing. If that's not enough for you, I have a final tip for you. Trying it out is at your own risk!

If you are not one hundred percent satisfied with any part of your body, then just visit an outdoor pool in the summer. The physical inadequacies offered here exceed even the wildest expectations. Incidentally, I don't think that's bad at all, on the contrary. It's just the real world and not the one in the glossy magazines or movies. What surprises me regularly, however, is the self-confidence and self-confidence with which, for example, the owners of a huge beer pug proudly flaunt it - and generally without a T-shirt over it. Why is it that most of the time it is exactly the people who run around with bare chests that you don't want to see? And why do those who you would like to take a closer look at wear Dresses with a high-necked Peter Pan collar? Only for the toughest: there is still the nudist beach. However, I haven't dared to do that yet. You want to sleep peacefully at night ...

But back to the principle of contrast: this usually involves very subtle methods that work in one way or another for each of us. What does a cunning salesman do when he wants to make us spend a lot of money? If he uses the contrast principle, he does the following: He shows us the most expensive product first and then the cheaper ones. Robert B. Cialdini describes this tactic using the example of a men's outfitter. Suppose a man wants to buy a suit and shirt. The best way for staff to sell is when they first offer the expensive suit and then the shirt. That can be expensive in that case, regardless. In any case, it is cheaper compared to a suit. The chances that both pieces will be bought are higher if this order is followed than if the shirt and then the suit were offered. In that case, the contrast principle would even work against the seller, because if we first see a cheaper product and then an expensive one, the expensive goods inevitably seem even more expensive to us. The energy follows the attention, in both directions.

Car salespeople often use the principle by first negotiating the price of the car with their customers and then quoting the prices for the extras. If we spend thousands of euros on a car, then hundreds of amounts suddenly seem puny, even though, objectively speaking, we are currently spending a lot of money. A few years ago I bought a car and a bike in one day. The bike dealer was lucky. After spending a lot of money on a car, the few hundred euros for the bike seemed like a bargain price to me. Under normal circumstances, I would not have just bought the expensive bike, but in that case I used the contrast principle. Let us now deal with the categories mentioned by Robert B. Cialdini in detail.

Reciprocity pays off

"Nothing costs more than what is available for free," is how Michihiro Matsumoto sums it up. Next December you can get an idea of how reliably the reciprocity rule works. Just grab the phone book and send Christmas cards to complete strangers. You will see that in the following weeks you will suddenly receive a lot of mail.

This is exactly what the researchers Philipp Kunz and Michael Woolcott did in 1976. The result was astounding. Almost all of the people they wrote had replied - without even wanting to know from whom they had actually received the card. At some point you got mail and just replied to it. Completely automatically. Stimulus and reaction, a logical consequence. This brings us to Robert B. Cialdini's rule of reciprocity: «This rule says that we should endeavor to give back to others what we have received from them. If someone does us a favor, we should do him a favor too… ”This need to return favors promptly appears to run through all cultures. However, with time and sufficient distance to the impulse it decreases more and more, as long as it is only a small favor. So if a stranger offered you chewing gum five years ago, you are not necessarily going to suddenly donate one of your kidneys to him. On the other hand, if someone really did you a big favor five years ago, you will not forget it and react accordingly, even if you have to invest a lot for it. Incidentally, this applies not only to favors, but also vice versa for everything bad that happens to us. It is already in the Bible: "We reap what we sow." If someone really did you a great favor five years ago, you will remember it and act accordingly, even if you will have to put a lot of effort into it. Incidentally, this applies not only to favors, but also vice versa for everything bad that happens to us. It is already in the

Bible: "We reap what we sow." If someone really did you a great favor five years ago, you will remember it and act accordingly, even if you will have to put a lot of effort into it. Incidentally, this applies not only to favors, but also vice versa for everything bad that happens to us. It is already in the Bible: "We reap what we sow."

Before I become too grand, a few examples from everyday life: Studies have shown that questionnaires are much more likely to be sent back to the sender if the respondents not only receive the questions but also a small gift of money. Since we all prefer to hold the sparrow in our hand than to see the pigeon on the roof, it makes sense for companies to send their surveys directly with a voucher for a smaller amount, for example. An insurance customer satisfaction questionnaire sent with a five-dollar check is twice as effective as offering to reward completed questionnaires with fifty dollars (Warriner, Goyder, Gjertsen, Horner, and McSpurren, 1996).

Another study shows that customers tip more when they have a small piece of candy added to their bill (Strohmetz, Rind, Fisher and Lynn, 2002). Free samples that are available in stores also fall into this category. Vance Packard writes in his famous book "The Secret Seducers" from the fifties - for me the book about sales and advertising, by the way, although it's already so old - about a salesman who sold the entire range of cheeses in the supermarket within a few hours because he offered its customers to cut off free samples for themselves.

The perfidious thing is that the automatism works with us even if the favors have not been requested from us at all beforehand. And even people we don't like can ingratiate themselves with us by showing off with a little good deed. Even then, we feel obliged to respond to this advance payment. In short: this rule restricts us in our decision-making behavior, because usually only those who are the first to do someone a favor can decide freely. He determines what favor he will do us and he will determine what consideration he wants to ask from us.

Incidentally, the same also applies in price negotiations in which one party specifies the amount. Suppose you want to buy a product. The first thing the seller says is his - in your opinion overpriced - price, let's say one hundred euros. You think that this is not a reasonable request and you offer eighty euros. Common sense usually leads us to meet in the middle and come to an agreement with the first bidder. The product changes hands for ninety euros. Why actually? In reality there is no reason for it, is there?

I still have some good news for you: the rule of reciprocity does not apply in our family and should not apply to friends either. Especially from good friends we accept favors without ifs and buts and without getting a guilty conscience or feeling our duty. In family and with real friends, people usually help each other because they like each other. And for no other reason. Maybe you think so too.

A modification of this rule is a concession. One evening my son wanted to have another chocolate bar. I didn't allow him to do that at first. But he still got a small piece. This can happen to us in other areas as well. This is also called the door-in-the-face tactic. It's very simple: we are asked a huge favor that we do not want to fulfill. After we have rejected the favor, the other person asks us for a smaller favor - if they really want to manipulate us by the line and thread, then the smaller concern may be exactly what they had in mind from the beginning. The chance that we will give in to this request now is extremely high. The contrast principle is used again here.

On my last evening entertainment there was a moment when I tried to borrow a bank note. A few years ago I always said at this point: "Next I need a banknote!" But that was a long time ago, a typical beginner's mistake. Nobody feels addressed in this way. The result: no one responded. Then I read from Robert B. Cialdini about the principle of contrast, reciprocity and the magic of concessions. Then I tried the following variant to influence my audience. I pointed to a man in the audience and said: "Next I need a hundred marks." It really was a long time ago, back then there was no internet, no e-mails, no casting shows, no navigation systems - and no euros. The reaction now was mostly a nervous smile, so also in the case of the targeted gentleman. However, due to the peer pressure within the crowd, he always looked in his wallet.

We will discuss in more detail later why it is always more useful to address a single person from the crowd specifically and directly than simply addressing a general request to everyone. In the case described above, there were several options: Either he had a hundred-mark note with him and wanted to lend it to me, or he had a hundred-mark note with him and didn't want to lend it to me. Maybe he had less available - or more, whatever. Anyway, after the gentleman had checked my case, I paused and said: "Well, it doesn't have to be a hundred marks, twenty or ten is enough." These restrictions worked like pure magic. From that moment on, many spectators reached into their pockets and held up their bills. I still do this today in cases like this

At this point a tip for my young readers: If you want more pocket money, then try the following tactic: Let's say you get twelve euros a week and want to have fifteen euros in the future. The sums are chosen arbitrarily here; my children are so young that they don't even get any pocket money. The numbers at this point are pure placeholders. Well: You can drastically increase your chances if you go a little higher with your request for more pocket money. The best way to say it is: "Dearest dad, I just don't have enough pocket money. All my friends get eighteen euros. " If your dearest dad - or dearest mom - agrees now, I congratulate you. In that case, watch your face. The amazement shouldn't be too great, and neither should the joy that can be read in it. Show rather moderate joy and thank you. Don't talk too much now! Just say thank you from the bottom of your heart, collect the money and leave.

Assuming he then says no, you could still try it with fifteen euros. This tactic already has a permanent place in my evening program. Rightly. One more word of warning: If you set your first demand disproportionately high, i.e. too high, the shot may backfire. In such cases, the request will be viewed as unrealistic or outrageous, which will rub off on your reputation. You will no longer be taken seriously. A person with good negotiating skills will choose his claim in such a way that it leaves room for the offer of the other side. If he operates skillfully, he will get - as a concession - exactly the offer from the other side that he supposedly had in mind the whole time anyway. But only if the other side has not read this book ... At this point I could quote many other fine examples from Robert B. Cialdini. But I don't do that and prefer to look for my own. If you want to read more of him, the book The Psychology of Persuasion is full of it, and it is really worth reading.

One more word about the skillful defense of the method. It is not necessary to decline all free offers, samples, and favors just to avoid being influenced. If you want, please take the offer. But you should change your point of view and from now on see all these gifts no longer as presents, but as a detail of a sales trick. You will no longer feel indebted to the giver. He wants to do business with you and you are free to accept or decline. With that in mind, nothing can happen to you. It is the same with the concession. Once you understand the tactic, you can think what you want, according to the title of this book. I could also say again: The world is what you think it is.

Another story shows very clearly how the principle of contrast can work in the right hands. The story is about one of the most dazzling con artists in history: Victor Lustig. He even managed to sell the Eiffel Tower to some bona fide junk dealers! But that's a different story. Here is his application of the principle of contrast: The matter shows that even Al Capone was not safe from this method.

Lustig just went to Capone and told him he could double the $ 50,000 for him if he could just lend him that money. Since Lustig had very good manners, looked very well-groomed and spoke perfect English, Capone gave him the sum. The deal was that Capone should get double that back in sixty days. But Lustig took the money, put it in a bank safe and drove to New York to "work" there. The money stayed there for two months without Lustig or anyone else being interested in it. Funny hadn't even touched the money. After sixty days, Lustig took the money out of the safe and went back to Capone. He smiled kindly and said apologetically that he hadn't been able to double the money he borrowed. He was really sorry he had failed.

Capone reacted visibly angry. He immediately thought about how and by whom he could have Lustig killed. Then something surprising happened. Lustig took the $ 50,000 out of his pocket and gave it back to Capone. It was $ 50,000, of course, the exact same money Capone had given him two months earlier. He gave it to him with the words that he was infinitely sorry for his failure and that he would have loved to double the money, that he himself had desperately needed the business.

Capone was impressed. He had never expected to get twice as much - but he had expected even less to get the money back. With the words: "My God, are you honest," he gave Lustig $ 5,000 to help him out of trouble. He was very grateful and overwhelmed. After a deep bow, he left the room. That $ 5,000 had been Lustig's goal from the start. By the way, history also shows that kindness and sympathy are incredibly powerful manipulators.

Commitment and Consistency

In this case, commitment means something like "commit, commit, commit to something". Please don't be surprised that I translate a noun with a verb, I think it reads more fluently and hits the meaning better. "Determination, commitment and commitment" - these nouns sound a bit stilted. I think that is also the reason why the word "commitment" has established itself as a technical term in German and can also be found more and more often in the media.

In my "Blue Elephant" I described the so-called Monty Hall dilemma. You remember? In German it is sometimes called the goat problem. This shows that a person

233

has a tendency to continue to hold on to a decision that has been made. Even if you can prove to him that his decision might not be favorable, he remains unwavering.

The newspaper representative mentioned on page 24 et seq. Could clearly talk me into several subscriptions with the principle of consistency. From my point of view it would have been inconsistent not to buy the newspapers from him. After all, I had told him beforehand that I would like to read magazines and help someone at any time. Of course, we all want to keep our word and thus behave consistently. It is precisely this endeavor that makes the method such an effective weapon of influence. We don't want to appear fickle, this is exactly what cunning salespeople or fellow human beings could use and thus make us violate our interests, just to keep our image nicely polished so that we can continue to feel good.

Knowing about this can also help you to stop being stolen from on the beach or in the outdoor pool. In 1975, for example, the following situation was faked by two scientists (Moritary, 1975): Imagine a busy beach in summer: A beach visitor - in reality one of the researchers - spreads out his towel and puts his clothes, his bag and his portable radio next to him on the towel. Shortly afterwards he gets up and walks along the sea. Now a thief comes along - in reality the other researcher - and just takes the radio away. You can probably guess how most of the others reacted, namely not at all. They just looked away. Out of twenty people, only four made efforts to prevent the theft.

Before you start believing that people are just all bad, please read on. With a simple trick, nineteen out of twenty people could be tricked into disturbing a thief. Before the researcher sets out for a walk, he simply says to the other beach guests: "I'll be gone for a moment, would you please take care of my things?" If the thief comes now, almost everyone who is spoken to has an eye on the radio and is immediately active.

Why we charlatans like to be pestered so much

The rule of commitment and consistency is also one of the reasons why people are generally so magically attracted to miracle healers, the media and charlatans. In order to make this statement clear to you, I have to go back a little.

It makes our lives a lot easier if we hold on to an opinion once we have formed it! That reads cynically, but it is not meant that way at all. We have to think and decide so much in order to cope with our everyday life, grapple with masses of information and then filter out exactly which of it is relevant for us. Since we can get a maximum of nine and at least five impressions out of all the information anyway, it makes a lot of sense that we have a kind of energy-saving mode in our head that makes it easier for us to think. Nature has arranged it in the best way that it has given us a mechanism to better cope with the complexity of our everyday life. So the consistency doesn't just have disadvantages. However, if someone takes advantage of them, it can have severe consequences for us.

Let's further assume that someone has a really profound concern about losing a loved one. The person concerned would do anything to be able to talk to him again. Now someone comes along and claims that he can actually arrange that and get in touch with the dead person. The desire for this offer to work is so strong that it is seriously considered to accept it. But with that we have already committed ourselves! The first step into the consistency trap has been taken.

As soon as someone is caught up in the seductive offer of a medium or miracle healer, it becomes very difficult - due to the commitment and consistency - to convince them that this is all just nonsense. After the first session, this is almost no longer possible, even with very good arguments.

A sentence that I hear again and again when I express myself skeptically in this regard is: "Now please explain to me how ..." Then comes a really incredible story. To be honest, I always feel a little uncomfortable. I know that effectiveness is the measure of the truth and it really helps many people to have a lucky charm in their pocket or to go to a responsible fortune-teller. In my private life I actually much prefer to talk about music, guitars, beautiful cars or good series - by the way, the best in my opinion is still "The Sopranos". Some acquaintances, however, always like to talk about their experiences with the psychic. I can understand that - the topic is so appealing that I've built part of my professional career on it. It's a fascinating thing I like to admit that. Still, I don't like to explain some things. The mentalist Joseph Dunninger once said: "For those who believe in it, no explanation is necessary, and for those who do not believe in it, no explanation is enough." It is exactly like that. The saying works both ways: those who firmly believe in it will take no arguments against it, and others do not need to put forward any arguments.

When asked: "Now please explain this to me ...", a story usually follows that really cannot be explained. This can have many reasons. One of them is that it may be a story that happened to a work colleague of the brother-in-law's sister. Because it is so good, it has of course been passed on so often that its content is now very far from the truth. The famous spider in the yucca palm! When retelling, we don't remember many details completely and so an orally transmitted story turns into a completely different story after a few instances - as with the silent post. In case you can't understand the details: Answer the following question - without looking up - how many pillars does the Brandenburg Gate have? By the way: It can be seen on the German fifty cents. We have it in hand every day.

Incidentally, I am not an outspoken skeptic myself. I believe in many unprovable things, provided that they work for me. Call it the placebo effect for me - that's fine with me. "Effectiveness is the measure of truth." You already know!

But why do people so-called miracle healers or media stick to their lips? And why do they defend their point of view all the more vehemently, the better the arguments of the other side get? The answer: Above all, commitment and consistency are at play here. As soon as we have seriously sought advice from such a person, we remain consistent so as not to appear like weirdos in front of our fellow human beings. We all try to justify ourselves again and again to others and to ourselves. The harder the headwind, the stronger our urge to punch through our position. It's not always wise, but it is very human. And then things take their course.

Who writes stays

"The weakest ink is better than the best memory," goes a Chinese proverb. Like everything else, this knowledge also has a special aspect that we can make use of. That means: If you really want to achieve something, then it helps immensely to just write down these goals. Commitments that we make for ourselves also work better. That is one reason why projects written down on paper are pursued with more energy than simply dreamed of. Likewise, talking to friends about your goals is a good thing. We make a binding commitment. As I recently read in the newspaper Die Welt, this can even be used by people with test anxiety: "Psychology - Overcoming test anxiety. A current study »in the journal Science shows that a short writing exercise can help, especially if the person has acute test anxiety. In one attempt, half of the participants were asked to write a short text about their own fears about the exam, while the others sit quietly or write about other non-exam-related events. The former performed better in the subsequent test (Die Welt, 2011).

When looking at a shooting star, we like to wish for something - a beautiful ritual. However, we advise our children not to talk to anyone about their wish - otherwise it will not come true. That makes things more mysterious, but if we're honest, that's a lot of nonsense, of course. Why should a wish come true at all just because I haven't talked to anyone about it? The opposite is the case! So I do it differently with my children. I let them tell me about their wishes - if they want to tell me. By the way, I never tell them whether I think the wish will come true or not. Wishes can be so powerful that I don't want to nip that power in the bud with my unfavorable comments. That's part of the power of authority which we will come to later on. Even if my older daughter wishes to become a mermaid as soon as she swims in Lake Starnberg, or if my son longs for a house kite - I'll save an obvious joke at this point - and my little one wants to be able to talk to all animals: Who am I to be allowed to downplay such beautiful wishes? So I keep silent and am happy about such creative dreams. that I can downplay such beautiful wishes? So I keep silent and am happy about such creative dreams. that I can downplay such beautiful wishes? So I keep silent and am happy about such creative dreams.

I have good news for you

How many times have we heard the following two sentences: «I have two messages for you, a good one and a bad one. Which one do you want to hear first? " That brings me to a question, dear reader: What message should you convey first? As you can imagine, the order has a considerable influence on the future state of your counterpart. Just think about the commitment and consistency rule for a moment before you answer!

Perhaps the following example will help you along the way: Robert B. Cialdini describes it in a study that he carried out in 1978 with John Cacioppo, Rod Basset and John Miller. It was about professors trying to get students to get up at seven in the morning to take part in an experiment on thought processes. Here is the progression in Robert B. Cialdini's words: "We immediately informed some of the students whom we contacted by phone about the time of the experiment. Of these, only twenty-four percent said they would participate. In another part of the sample, we used the low-ball tactic: we first asked if they wanted to participate in a study of thought processes, and only after they answered (56 percent yes), we mentioned the starting time of seven o'clock and gave them the opportunity to withdraw their commitments at any time, which none of the students did. It goes even further: Ninety-five percent of them kept their promise and, as promised, appeared at seven in the morning in the psychology building of the university »(Robert B. Cialdini, 1997).

Low ball tactic means that you offer someone a deal or ask for something and only add an unpleasant aspect after the acceptance. Due to the principle of consistency, the person concerned will most likely stick with the promised deal despite the restriction. This is high school manipulation. The consequence is clear:

Always, always, always bring the good news first.

To protect yourself against attacks of this kind, there is a good trick: just think about it! Once all the facts are on the table, do you really weigh everything up: "Now that I know everything about this matter, would I make my decisions again as I did without this knowledge?" So after I realized that the supposedly poor East German newspaper seller was not just doing a harmless survey, but wanted to talk me into a subscription, would I make the same decision as before? No. From the moment the cat was out of the bag, I should have spoken plainly and revised my opinion: "You stole my time under the wrong auspices. You don't do a survey, you sell magazines. You start your conversation with a lie. I don't want to do business with people like you. Goodbye." When I was eighteen I probably wouldn't have dared to do it. It's different today. And the paradox about it: The moment you face a manipulator so resolutely, you have his respect. The moment you fall for his scam and do what he wants from us, you have lost all respect.

Social proven or eternal greets the groundhog

Brian: "You are all individuals." - Mass: «Yes, we are all individuals!» - Brian: "And you are all completely different!" - crowd: "Yes, we are all completely different!" - One: "Not me!" This dialogue comes from the film "The Life of Brian". His statement aims to ensure that when we make a decision, we often base our decisions on what others expect and believe to be right. True to the motto: So many people can't be wrong. If everyone does something, then there must be something to it.

One evening I was able to admire this principle in practice at one of my favorite home shopping stations, "HSE 24". Here you can order anything and have it sent to your home. A groundbreaking, completely new type of fitness machine has just been touted. Among other things, people were constantly having their say who had lost several pounds in a very short time with this part. Furthermore, it was emphasized again and again how many people - I think there were tens of thousands - with this miracle machine mutated from the ugly sister of Mickey Rourke to the beautiful twin sister of Heidi Klum. All of this, of course, within a few weeks and without any effort. So advertising primarily took advantage of the assumption that we think something would be true if many others had experienced it and could confirm it.

By the way, because they have proven themselves socially, the so-called urban legends cannot be crushed either. Incredible stories, bizarre ghost stories and barely comprehensible conspiracy theories are constantly being told. For me the most astonishing phenomenon is that with each further story they get wilder and wilder. In addition, more and more people take them at face value the longer they persist in circulation. That's the way it is: rumors that are repeated often are more believed than true stories that are not mentioned as often. Repetition is about truth. Can't so many really be wrong? Yes, they can.

For example, until recently, I myself believed that the Inuit had up to fifty words for snow. Then the editors of "Bayern 2" explained to me. The Inuit don't have more words for snow than the Germans. According to an article in the Süddeutsche Zeitung, they have no less than two words for snow.

This urban legend shows how much one can be misled when many talk about something. After all, you can't check everything and too often you trust that the information is correct. Especially when even anthropologists, linguists and scientists speak of it and such comments are published in well-known newspapers and even school books. Still, a lot is just not right! Proven! Although it seems so logical.

Mostly it has been argued that Inuit had so many words for snow because it was useful for them to differentiate in their surroundings. That sounds reasonable, but it's nonsense. Conversely, one could think that the Germans would have fifty words for house. After all, houses shape our landscape to the same extent as snow does the Inuit environment. Still, we don't have fifty words for it. We use compounds to make our distinctions. So we speak of high-rise, duplex, farmhouse, apartment building, wooden house, etc. They are also called compound nouns - so, I just had to write that now. But back to the topic: You see, just because many people believe something, objectively speaking, it is far from true.

I myself recently fell into exactly this trap. A customer booked me for an annual meeting in Kassel. My lecture was scheduled for four o'clock. Nevertheless, I should arrive the evening before. That amazed me, because my presentation does not require a high technical effort or a lot of preparation. Even so, the customer insisted. I told him that I really didn't think it was necessary. "We do a lot of events, and all artists do it that way!" Was his clear statement.

These words were his magic formula: social reliability. The day before I traveled from Munich to Kassel, stayed in a shabby hotel, but submitted to my fate. When I asked about the possibility of having something to eat, the receptionist replied: "If you still want to eat something, you can walk in that direction for five minutes and a gas station will come. You might get a few more Viennese there. " Yes, I can still be amazed. The next morning, after a short night, the agency representative greeted me with the words: "Oh, Mr. Havener, you are already here. Your performance is only in seven hours. " At that moment I fell into a deep trance. You see, as an old fox, I still fall for such things sometimes.

I'll give you another example: when I'm on tour, my team and I naturally drive a lot. So it is inevitable that we sometimes go to a toilet at motorway service stations. Here mostly a woman sits at a little table with a small plate on which there are coins. But there are never ten or twenty cents on these plates, no, it always starts at fifty cents. So here it is pointed out - without saying it - that a visit to this facility should be worth at least fifty cents.

Speaker and trainer Cavett Robert once said: "Since ninety-five percent of people are copycats and only five percent are leaders, people are more persuaded by actions than by any other argument." As soon as Michelle Obama buys a dress at H&M and is photographed, it becomes a bestseller (Die Bunte, 2011). The girls run into them and the dress has to be produced in large numbers again and again. But before we scold the oh-so-stupid Americans: After Prince William's engagement with Kate

Middleton, the same phenomenon was triggered in England. The clothing and jewelry industry in Great Britain was delighted. Everyone wanted the blue sapphire and the matching dress. So: stupid Americans and stupid English? No,

Here, too, the principle applies again: "The energy follows the attention"; it can be used successfully to sell something to others or to lure them out of their pockets.

The trick can also be used to help other people. Robert B. Cialdini describes a strategy with which children who suffered from long-term anxiety could drastically reduce precisely these anxieties. Preschool children who were disproportionately afraid of dogs were selected for a test. These children were simply asked to watch a boy of their own age play with a dog for twenty minutes. After just four days, sixty-seven percent of those affected agreed to go to the dog and pet it. The fear of the animals did not come back either.

In a second study, the researchers showed children a film in which several peers played with a dog. As a result, the result could even be increased: the more people provide obvious evidence for something, the more the principle applies to us, so the logical conclusion.

Psychologist Robert O'Connor conducted a similar study in 1972. This case concerned over-anxious preschoolers. About those who always stand on the edge of the school yard when everyone else is playing together. Those who in my generation always wore cords or dungarees in kindergarten. Unfortunately, this fear - unlike the spread of corduroy and dungarees - has hardly decreased to this day. For the shy ones, O'Connor made a film set in a kindergarten. It is always about outsiders joining a group with the children playing at the end of a scene and suddenly taking part in the game. He showed these sequences to the anxious children. The effect was enormous: after the children in question had seen the film,

The long-term effect of the film is even more astonishing: the outsiders who hadn't seen it were just as isolated after six weeks as before, whereas the children who knew it were in some cases even able to develop into the most active group members. The film lasted only twenty-three minutes and the children had only seen it once - but its impact was so convincing because it lasted.

In this context, it is important to note that the same film would not have worked with children if it had shown adults joining a group or playing with dogs. The principle is most seductive when the protagonists are similar to ourselves. The more similar the group is to us, the stronger the influence on us. So this principle has an enormous effect.

All clubs founded by people who drive the same make of car or play the same instrument work on the principle of similarity. Interest in one and the same thing first makes us sympathetic to the other. Of course, it can later turn out that there are a lot of members in our club who are not at all suitable for us, but we will definitely address those with whom we feel we have something in common. Otherwise we could never get into conversation and each other. All sorts of groups - like the punks in the eighties or the counter-movement to it, the poppers - have come together in this way.

As a schoolboy I once had an argument with a classmate whom I had only met as an idiot before. However, when I found out that he had pretty much the same taste in music as I did, I suddenly had great difficulty finding him still stupid. Somehow I soon got into conversation with him, he suddenly attracted me magically. Then I changed my opinion about him a little, but not really fundamentally and lastingly - he was just really an idiot ... And yet: Without the same taste in music we would not have gotten to talk shop.

Other things - like the same birthday or place of birth - also increase the likelihood values. Imagine meeting a stranger and it turned out that he was born on the same day as you. The likelihood that you will do this exact person a favor is already higher after receiving this message than it was before.

The whole thing only works through commonality. And that's just one thing. As soon as you find out that you still have a mutual friend with your new acquaintance, increase the sympathy values again.

How much sympathy is controlled by external factors became clear to me once more when I attended a medieval knight tournament. That took place in a large arena. The audience was divided into several groups. Each group got its knight. Although the assignment was completely arbitrary, a common ground immediately arose with those seated around me. Believe it or not, we agreed within seconds - without exchanging a word - and only cheered for our knight and booed the other comrades-in-arms. The experience made me quite pensive. In such a short time it was possible to influence so many people with one sentence and everyone followed the figure of identification as if led by an invisible hand.

The chapter on rapport tells you how to gain understanding yourself and how to come across as personable. I have already described why unfriendly people, even if they should be right and only have good arguments, are always worse off than friendly people. Even if they only have weak arguments and are actually wrong.

If the members of two parties meet on a talk show, the contrast principle applies first of all (see page 119). But another aspect comes into play immediately: because one attribute of a person allows us to infer several others. That's why we're usually in a pretty bad position when we deliver bad news. The negative information infects us in this case. An old wisdom. For this reason, charlatans always have an easy game.

Because they only promise good things: "I can talk to a dead person who is close to you, I have the solution to your problem, I'll make you rich, I'll make you happy, I'll make you slim, etc." Each of us has our weak points. And as soon as they are addressed with such a sentence, it is very seductive to blindly follow this savior.

Advertising also constantly uses the principle of association: beautiful people drive beautiful cars, beautiful people are right: Heidi Klum eats at McDonald's and Verona Pooth helps the 11880. Can you imagine that men judge a car to be faster as soon as it opens the advertising poster next to the car shows an attractive woman? It's really like that. At that moment, they switch off their brains and only let their emotions speak.

Of course, the whole thing also works in the other direction: A thing is not only rated as more attractive if it is associated with a beautiful person or a person who is popular. For example, you can come across as more personable if you give someone a nice experience. It doesn't have to be something incredibly original. An invitation to dinner is enough. And already the good clings to you. Everyone who has ever been deeply in love knows that. The first meeting where you really get closer usually takes place in a nice restaurant where you can eat deliciously. This is the ideal place. This also works when collecting donations or asking for other favors. For this very reason, donations at galas are only collected after the menu. Why? On the one hand the principle of reciprocity applies here, on the other hand the strategy of association. A holistic tactic that even has a fitting name: snack technology.

It is often very difficult to evade someone's expressions of sympathy. We all want to be liked. In such moments there is only one possibility: to take a step back and ask yourself: "Why do I like this person so extraordinarily? Did he compliment me, do I have something in common with him, did he give me something to eat? " If that is the case, then make yourself aware that his product or claim has nothing to do with his expression of sympathy. Get rid of it, even if it's difficult. In the moment, concentrate fully on the thing and not on the person.

authority

Do you remember how my hypnosis teacher introduced me to a test audience? He said, "Now see one of the best known and best hypnotists I know." That was an outright lie, the gig in question was the first of its kind for me, I had never tried hypnotizing before. My teacher at the time just used the principle of authority. If someone is good at something or has a high status, then we believe these signals and automatically follow his instructions. The fact that my teacher at the time introduced me to the audience was enough. The test subjects were easily hypnotized because they thought I was a master and immediately accepted this fact.

According to the principle of association, a few good status symbols are enough to give someone authority. As soon as a man wears tailor-made suits, drives expensive sports cars and holds a doctorate, such externalities - which incidentally hardly reveal anything about his real character - have a lasting effect on us. It has nothing to do with superficiality. We all fall for it without exception and recognize authorities even in anticipatory obedience as soon as we notice the slightest sign. If you think that you will almost never fall for the outside world, then you should be extra careful now. The fact is that almost all people underestimate the influence of authority on their own behavior. Welcome to the club.

Robert B. Cialdini cites a very well-known study in this regard, in which a white coat and a professorial title led people to administer very painful and dangerous electric shocks to helpless people. The experiment was carried out at Yale in 1974 and went down in history as the "Milgram Experiment".

Milgram experiment

The experiment went as follows: A newspaper advertisement was sought for contributors to a memory experiment. Arriving at the laboratory, the participants met a professor - with title, smock and clipboard in hand - and another contributor. After the greeting, the test to be carried out is explained to them as follows: "It is about the effect of punishment on the learning process." The second test person - an actor, which is of course a secret - is given a list of pairs of terms with the task of memorizing them. So she takes on the role of the student. The first test person is given the task of querying the knowledge later and thus has the role of the teacher. So after memorizing the list, the student is seated on a chair and strapped into it. He has no way of getting up. Electrodes are also attached to his arm.

Now the teacher and professor go into the next room.

The student is now queried. For every wrong answer he gets an electric shock from the teacher. The spicy thing: After every wrong answer, the voltage is increased. After a few wrong answers, the power surges become excruciatingly painful. The student begs the professor to stop the experiment. But he insists on continuation. After further wrong answers and electric shocks, the student writhes in pain in the chair and cries out loudly. Whimpering, he asks to stop the experiment. At the professor's command, further power surges follow mercilessly - with up to three hundred volts. Even when the student no longer answers, the professor orders that the lack of response be interpreted as a mistake and that the electric shocks continue. To the bitter end …

This cruel study was carried out in exactly the same way. In reality, it wasn't about checking learning behavior either. It was about examining the power of authorities. What do people do to an innocent person, how far do they go when they are acting on behalf of an authority? The result was extremely worrying: In reality, the student had not received any electric shocks. It was just an actor playing it. Actually, the teacher was also tested - the person who administered the electric shocks on the orders of the professor.

The result: two thirds of the test persons fulfilled their assignment - mercilessly, to the bitter end. Only a third showed compassion and at a certain point refused to give the alleged student any further electric shocks. The study was also carried out on average people who had never before been noticed by anything violent in their life. "The most important finding of the investigation is to see the willingness of adults to do almost anything an authority asks them to do" (Milgram, 1974).

Originally, Milgram had wanted to investigate how it was possible that so many people in Germany had obeyed the horrific orders of the National Socialists. He wanted to check their level of obedience and make it understandable. However, after he had initially carried out the study in Yale, he came to the conclusion that he could save himself the flight to Germany. In America the participants obeyed so unconditionally that Milgram found it superfluous to substantiate his findings again in Germany.

In short, whatever is required of an authority is taken seriously by us and we follow it. This is because we were urged to obey from childhood: Listen to your mom, your dad, your grandma, your grandpa, your teacher ... In this way, a conditioning takes place in our head as soon as we come across a supposed authority face. This mechanism is of course important for the functioning of a society. Up to a certain point. In emergencies, for example, it can be very useful to follow those responsible.

It becomes cruel the moment the authority is up to bad things: Churchmen or teachers exploit their authority, abuse children and then try to cover up their deeds. Ministers adorn themselves with false doctorates, and impostors put on white coats and operate on open hearts without a license to practice medicine. The power of the authorities, including the bad, is omnipresent. And so it comes to the most bizarre situations.

Investigations in hospitals, for example, have shown that the nursing staff will follow the instructions of the senior doctor even if they know that the order is incorrect. Irresponsible doses of medication have even been administered and, in one very bizarre case, eye drops have been dripped into a patient's bottom just because the chief doctor supposedly wanted them to. This case went down in medical history under the name of "rectal earache".

Goethe endangers your health

That works and is a correct statement, as Johann Wolfgang von Goethe himself was able to prove in 1774: In his book "Quirkology" the author Richard Wiseman describes the effect of the novel "The Sorrows of Young Werther" on society at the time of the great poet.

The key work of the Sturm und Drang period is about a young man who falls in love with a woman who, however, has already been promised to someone else. Werther loves her so much that he takes his own life because he knows: Your love will never have a chance. The book became a huge success after it was published. It is written so thrillingly that after reading it, rows and rows of young unhappily in love took their own lives. Eventually, so many young people committed suicide in exuberance that the work was banned.

Since then, the phenomenon has been the subject of controversy in science. Some speak of a downright epidemic, while others think that everything was not so wild. There is evidence of a double-digit number of suicides that were directly related to the book. Some of the suicides had dressed exactly like Werther in the book: blue tailcoat, yellow waistcoat, yellow breeches, boots and gray hat. Incidentally, the Goethe actor wears exactly the same clothing most of the time in "Goethe!". For me, this film is once again good proof that German directors can make very good films. But back to the subject: some suicides still had the book in hand.

The term "Werther Effect" was introduced in 1974 by the American sociologist David Phillipps. He had examined the coverage of suicides by well-known people and their impact on the suicide rate on the population. In all of the cases he consulted, he was able to determine an increase.

In the eighties, the multi-part series "Tod einer Schülers" was shown on German television. In six episodes, the history of a student's suicide was told from different perspectives. The suicide rate among fifteen to nineteen year olds increased by one hundred and seventy-five percent after it was broadcast. After the repetition, the suicide rate rose again by one hundred and fifteen percent. Incomprehensible! Even in the United States, according to media reports, the number of suicides rose by thirty percent within two weeks. Especially as soon as celebrities and popular figures and their fate were reported, the clear influence was noticed. For example, in the United States, the suicide rate rose twelve percent even after the death of Marilyn Monroe.

For this reason, even the German Press Council asks in its statutes for restraint when it comes to reporting on suicides. The more details are made public, the more imitators there are. We know that by now. For this reason, names, places and accompanying circumstances are usually never mentioned in the newspapers. That is the dark side of social validity. So similarity is a factor that plays a big role here. The second quantity, as we shall see in a moment, is uncertainty.

A paragraph that can save lives

According to Robert B. Cialdini, this is perhaps the most important finding that can be derived from his research: The principle of social reliability aims at the fact that people always orientate themselves towards what their environment is doing. This is exactly the reason why it is possible for people to be beaten to death on the street or in suburban trains or suddenly have a heart attack without anyone bothering to do so.

The paradox of this situation: the more people witness such an event, the less likely it is that someone will intervene. Everyone just looks at the reaction of the other observers. If no one is courageous and takes the initiative, nothing at all happens. But this is not due to a lack of compassion or is even malice - no, the reason is to be seen solely in the insecurity of most people who feel overwhelmed by such a situation. As soon as an individual becomes active, the ice is broken and the first domino falls. Suddenly many others are helping too.

I do not wish any of my readers to ever get into such a threatening situation, but if you do get into trouble on a busy street, the very knowledge - that the failure to provide assistance is based on sheer uncertainty - can help you out of possible difficulties. The trick is not to let any uncertainties arise in the first place. Assuming you notice in the S-Bahn that you are getting very strange, then you speak to one person from the crowd of passengers. As a rule, they will immediately feel responsible and take action. Because she knows that she is meant. That must be clear in any case. So it is best to say: "You in the red jacket with the blond hair, I need your help because I have the feeling that I am about to break down. Please call an ambulance." With this procedure you can remove any uncertainties out of the way. But only if a person with a red jacket and blond hair is present. So you shouldn't memorize this sentence. Please describe the person who, of all those present, appears to you to be the most suitable to help you! The person concerned notices that they are meant, they have received a clear assignment from you. This way, you drastically increase your chances of having someone by your side. which of all those present seems to you the most suitable to help you! The person concerned notices that they are meant, they have received a clear assignment from you. This way, you drastically increase your chances of having someone by your side. which of all those present seems to you the most suitable to help you! The person concerned notices that they are meant, they have received a clear assignment from you. This way, you drastically increase your chances of having someone by your side.

Really likeable!

A few months ago I was a guest at "People at Maischberger". The theme of the program: "Supernatural powers: mystery or nonsense?" Imagine the following scenario: On the one hand the front of the absolute opponents of everything that has anything to do with esoteric ideas, on the other hand there were the media, esotericists and doctors who swear by alternative healing methods. I was sitting somewhere in the middle. For me, the show was a real highlight for polemics and senseless debates. Statements such as "I can communicate with anyone who has died" - uttered by the medium Kim Anne Jannes - clashed with counterarguments such as: "There are two types of providers in the esoteric scene: Some are really convinced that they have supernatural abilities. The others know perfectly well that they can do nothing, but they do a real deal with the worries of others. " Some are cases for psychiatry, while others are for the public prosecutor, said Dr. Colin Goldner. Two worlds could not collide more violently. What both camps have in common, however, is their absolute view of the truth.

One faction claims that it can basically do anything in its field, the other argues that everyone who deals with this area is crazy or criminals. Viewed from the point of view of the rule of polarity, they give an interesting picture: Both camps are more similar than one might think at first glance. Viewed objectively, an absurd argument is refuted with an equally absurd counter-argument. The cat bites its tail and nothing moves and you can't go an inch. Both sides are biased and have a narrow view of the other's arguments. Exactly that contradicts the scientific claim that at least the anti-esoteric opponents claim for themselves. Real science can only come from an open mind, never from obstinacy. In my opinion, the truth can only be somewhere in between and not on either pole.

The principle of polarity says that every thing has two sides. Opposites are the poles of one and the same thing. In our example it is love and hate. Where there is love, there is quickly hostility. One faction is unconditionally absorbed in their life topic, the other despises their wisdom all the more. Everything ends in massive allegations. As soon as we move from the poles to the middle, the extreme emotions will eventually turn into affection or dislike. Further towards the center, "I like it" or "I don't like it so much" are located. All these evaluations are different degrees of the same thing according to the principle of polarity. The principle "Everything is one" applies.

I hope you will forgive me for digging a little back here in order to get my point across: one camp is just as stubborn as the other. Nobody is right and nobody is wrong.

All factions are prisoners of their ideologies and therefore behave in exactly the same way. Some do not question anything, others question everything except themselves. Some are vulnerable because of their absolute openness, others are vulnerable because of their absolute claim to truth. It no longer has anything to do with factual weighing. And both camps are exactly the same because they want to be so different - wonderfully paradoxical. Two facts about this appearance were noteworthy for me:

- After the recording in Cologne, I missed my flight to Nuremberg and instead was stuck at Düsseldorf airport for eight hours due to fog. Finally, I watched a full season of "Entourage" on my laptop and finally missed my appearance in Nuremberg. A first in my artistic career! I had never been late before, let alone not at all.

- The reactions of the TV viewers to the show quickly made it clear: The critics of the esoteric scene got off badly. Their opinion was devalued as forever yesterday and know-it-all. Even people from my circle of acquaintances, who actually have nothing to do with esotericism, found the representatives of this scene much friendlier and therefore followed their opinion more than the ranting tirades of the skeptics. They were easily upset, viciously insulted those who thought differently, and sometimes outraged and commented on their arguments, shaking their heads. The sentence was even heard: "A physicist doesn't think he knows." The esoteric followers reacted much more calmly. They were always friendly, collected, and calmly presented their arguments.

Imagine turning on the television. There you will see a group of people discussing with each other. Some insult, scold and gesticulate wildly - the others are under constant fire and always answer with caution. Which of the two camps do you like more?

That brings us to the topic: sympathy. My thesis: You will be more likely to convince and influence people who you think are nice than those who may have understandable, good arguments, but with whom you do not want to sit at the same table. Logical. It is clear to all of us that we prefer to be with someone who is also comfortable to us. Their opinion automatically applies more to us. You should know more about how this is possible in order to gain greater clarity about your own behavior in such situations. When do we like someone and when do we not?

People we like

Whether we like it or not, a lot of the unconscious influences the image we make of our counterpart. Prejudices and judgments, well balanced and quickly made. In your opinion, which person has the better general education: Sophie or Chantal? Please don't get me wrong, I have nothing against the two names, but I already know what you're going to say. In any case, none of my children are named Sophie or Chantal - especially not my son, which is why the answer will leave me cold.

We associate something with names and thus cultivate our clichés. At the end of the

1960s, researchers wanted to know how far these clichés go at this point. The result: people with unusual names were classified much more often as having psychological problems. The study also found that students with popular names in school were rated better by teachers than those with unpopular names. People with unpopular names are more likely to be socially isolated and more likely to suffer from inferiority complexes than those with common names (Hartmann, Nicolay, Hurley, 1968).

Fortunately, I didn't study in the USA until I was in my mid-twenties, at a time when I had already built up a bit of self-confidence, because Thorsten is a really impractical name in English-speaking countries - especially because of the "Th" at the beginning. By the way, scientists from the University of San Diego found that a person's initials can even affect life expectancy. They differentiated between people whose initials had a positive connotation - such as "Joy" for joy or "Hug" for hug - and people with initials with negative connotations such as "Pig" for pig and "die" for die. You know that in the US the middle name is often abbreviated, like John F. Kennedy, hence JFK. In addition, death certificates from California were evaluated using a database. The amazing result: Men with "positive" initials lived an average of four years longer, women three. According to the study, at least the bearers of "negative" initials had no disadvantages. They lived as long as the average, but no less. For this they took their own life particularly often!

These results show how much we all react subliminally to something that is with us all the time. Finally, apart from the words "yes" and "no", we hardly hear anything as often as our name. As we have just seen, it has a considerable influence on our attitude towards life and our actions. We can use this fact, for example we can give others a name that helps them. Imagine giving your child a nickname that has a positive connotation. Instead of choosing an unimaginative "little treasure", you could choose the name according to its inclinations. For example, my son is really into Indiana Jones. Not that he knows all the films, he's still a little short, but he's totally into this adventurer's image. I can understand that well. So I told my son that Indiana Jones was not only a great adventurer and treasure hunter, but also a very intelligent professor. Since then I've occasionally called him Dr. Jones. I think that's not only a nice nickname, but also a supportive one. It shows that I have a lot of confidence in him.

Another example: my grandmother had a twin sister. You must know that my grandma and I were very close. I even lived in an apartment below hers for many years and we always got along very well. At one point she and her sister complained to me about getting older. My girlfriend at the time - my current wife - and I then only called them the "Golden Girls". At some point they even called themselves that. This name surely made them more happy than "old boxes" and although it did not ignore their age, it added a little wink. The variant made us and them feel good and made our close relationship even closer. And all of this is only due to the fact that we infer many more from one characteristic, from a name to character traits.

Of course, a person's appearance also influences their impact on the environment. People who are less than 1.65 meters tall are not considered to be as productive as taller people. From a purely objective point of view, of course, this does not necessarily have to be correct. But that doesn't matter either. The mere fact that such an impression might influence a potential employer unnoticed is enough.

George Bush senior probably also knew about this effect. In the television duel in his presidential election campaign in 1988, for example, he shook hands with his opponent Michael Dukakis for an extremely long time. Rumor has it that this was a carefully devised strategy by his campaign team to document his physical superiority. Somewhere in our heads there is a program that means to us: taller people are more powerful, more productive, more resilient and also more attractive than smaller ones.

It looks bad for me here too. At 1.72 meters, I am at the bottom of the normal distribution scale for a man. I am aware of this every time I ask a male spectator to come to me on stage. They are almost always bigger than me. Well, that's the way it is.

This fact works both ways, by the way. Because we also think that capable people have to be great. That is nonsense, of course, but the prejudice is so stuck that you cannot simply refrain from it. But since the world is what we think it is, that is a fact that we have to accept. That even seems to be reflected in our bank account: A study by the University of Munich in 2004 was able to show that an additional centimeter in height brings on average 0.6 percent more to the gross monthly salary. In case you start pondering about your height: Nicolas Sarkozy, Dustin Hoffman, Tom Cruise and Madonna have achieved something too, although they are all less than 1.70 meters tall.

Now it is really astonishing: Depending on the attributes with which a person is presented to us, we estimate his size differently than it is objectively seen! When someone is introduced to us as an expert and a luminary, we consider them greater than a supposed loser or a good-for-nothing (Wilson, 1968). At a university, different groups of students were introduced to the same person with different titles and professions. Once you presented someone as a top scientist, once as a student, once as an assistant and once as a lecturer.

The higher the status of the presented person, the more impressive his height was perceived. The student was estimated at 1.72 meters - that is, thought to be less tall than he actually was, the professorial status alone made people grow ten centimeters to 1.82 meters. As I said: It was always one and the same person! In his book "Blink", Malcolm Gladwell describes how the presidential candidate Warren Harding was made president by zealous strippers in 1921 simply because of his attractive appearance. Historians agree that Harding is one of the worst presidents the US has ever had. Without his looks and his impressive height, he would never have been able to hold this office, would have been out of the question. The unjust fact The fact that archetypes - and, in our opinion, beautiful people - get more sympathy is called the Warren-Harding effect for this reason. The sight of an attractive person has a significant impact on our perception and thinking. As Gladwell puts it: "His appearance triggers so many associations that the normal thought process comes to a standstill."

I know other examples of this: In Western countries, clean-shaven men are considered more honest than those with a beard. Beards are associated with poor hygiene, cunning and dark machinations. Objectively speaking, this is nonsense, but effectiveness is again the measure of truth. In this context, compare the pictures of Saddam Hussein or Osama bin Laden with those of Guido Westerwelle or Angela Merkel. It's okay, the example of Ms. Merkel is a little joke. Everyone on Forbes' list of the hundred richest people in the world is clean-shaven, and no successful American presidential candidate has had a beard or mustache in a long time. A well-known politician in Germany had a mustache in the 1930s. In this case, unfortunately, the phenomenon could not prevent him from coming to power. On the contrary.

Good-looking men are also given much lower penalties by the courts than far less attractive ones (Stewart, 1980). Robert B. Cialdini describes cases where ugly defendants were jailed twice as often as pleasant-looking ones for the same offenses. Another study looked at the size of the fine in relation to the attractiveness of the accused. You already guessed it: the Gollums had to pay an average of $ 10,051, the handsome guys only $ 5,623. For the same type of violation of the law, mind you.

That is the dark side of influence. We know, of course, that a beautiful person is not automatically smarter, more honest or more productive - nevertheless we always fall for his appearance. This can have fatal consequences, you should keep that in mind. The best way to avoid falling for it, by the way, is still to mentally take a step back and remind yourself that this mechanism even exists. Then we should think carefully about whether we are falling for a subtle influence or not. But beauty is different for everyone.

Another factor in likeability is similarity. It is even one of the most important to convince the other person. The more similar a person is to us, the more likeable we will find them. The similarity can be expressed, for example, in outward appearances such as the similar style of clothing. Suppose you are fifty cents short to pay your fees at the parking meter: The best thing to do right now is to look out for someone who is dressed similarly to you. If that is exactly what you ask to lend you money, your chances of getting it are vastly higher.

Disenchantment of Authority

There is one thing you should definitely keep in mind if you want to become an impostor yourself: Never be too perfect. I can well imagine that when you read the first few examples in this section you thought: I'm not falling for expensive cars, suits and impressive titles! On the one hand, studies have shown that you do. And on the other hand, I quite deliberately stated that so unreservedly. Because I wanted you to be suspicious as you read it. As soon as someone applies too thick, we become cautious. To be too perfect is either boring or makes us sit up and take notice. In terms of the effect on others, neither is desirable. If someone is too perfect, they quickly come across as slimy or just make others jealous. And envy is something that we should neither feel ourselves nor evoke in others. Under no circumstances. If someone is jealous, they may invest a lot of time to find cracks in our facade. Small mistakes make us lovable and approachable. Never underestimate the destructive power of envy.

The philosopher Søren Kierkegaard put it this way: "Someone who admires and feels that he cannot be happy through devotion chooses to envy what he admires. So he soon speaks another language. In his language, what he actually admires means that it is nothing, that it is something stupid and embarrassing and strange and exaggerated. Admiration is happy self-disclosure, envy is unhappy self-assertion. "

I do not want to give a rating here regarding the behavior of those exposed and exposed. My advice is different: show weaknesses and openly admit at least one of them. As soon as letters of recommendation contain only positive comments, hiring managers become suspicious. However, if letters of recommendation also contain at least one less favorable comment about the applicant, this has a positive effect on the application (Knouse, 1983).

For you this means: admit weaknesses, talk about vices, even if the harmless ones. If somebody really digs through the dirt and finds something, then that reduces the height of your fall immensely. Robert Greene describes this very well in his «48 Laws of Power». He says: "Others can also come to money, just as they can come to power. But superior intelligence, good looks, charm -

those who do not have such qualities cannot acquire them either. Naturally perfect, those who are naturally perfect have to work the hardest to disguise their brilliance and show off a flaw or two to distract the envy before it settles in. It is a widespread naive misconception that one can please people with one's natural gifts: in reality, they will hate one for it »(Greene, 2006).

You can also use the power of authority for yourself in a roundabout way. For example, if you do not want to commit yourself, you can simply pass the decision on to the next higher authority. Suppose a customer calls you to negotiate the price of a quote. But you don't want to act. Instead of going on a confrontational course and telling the customer that there is no room for it, you can go about it in a gentle way and also gain understanding from your customer. Just tell them that you cannot make this decision on your own and that you need to discuss the matter with your manager. If you are the supervisor yourself, you can hire a co-manager. In either case, you must turn the search off to an authority. The then naturally rejects the request.

Do not underestimate this approach. The method will almost always be accepted by your counterpart. Even hostage-takers usually respond when the negotiator hands over responsibility to a superior. It also works very well at home: if my children want something that I don't want to go into, I can always say that I have to discuss it with their mother first. In the end, of course, she has the say.

I often ask the audience in my evening program not to believe everything. The skeptics present then always nod knowingly.

A few minutes later, however, I casually lead my audience on the ice with outrageous assertions that sound very credible. Many believe me everything until I confront them with the truth and confess that I just used a trick. This is where the power of authority is at play. In a convincing way. Interestingly, it is precisely at this point that there is a shift in reality. Because of my natural authority on stage, "normal" people usually believe everything, a little too much. They just want it that way. The magicians, on the other hand, assume that I work with tricks without exception - i.e. always -. But that is also not the truth. They regularly ask me how I managed to convict liars in articles for "Extra - the RTL magazine" or "Explosiv - das Magazin". They really want to know which magic trick I would have used here. The truth is often not believed in me: there is no magic trick at all. I used exactly the methods here that I have already described several times in my books. Finding the famous pin is exactly the same on my show. Many magicians want to know which trick I can use to find a needle hidden somewhere in the audience so quickly. There is nothing hidden about this number. The only secret is that I'm extremely focused

The person in authority also has great power when it comes to rapport: almost always the person with the higher status leads who follows with the lower status. If you want to meet someone on an equal footing, then you should proceed as described in the first chapter. Keep asking yourself how a supposed expert can benefit from the advice they give you. Additionally, ask yourself if you would trust the person if you knew them from a different perspective. Or if she wasn't introduced to you as an expert. It can also be very helpful to introduce yourself to the experts without your symbols of power - without a smock, suit or uniform and without a company car and title. Do you still trust this person? Or do you have doubts?

The scarcity of funds

I claim that my children have good table manners. They are polite, rarely speak with full mouths, show consideration for their siblings and their parents as long as there is enough of what they want. But as soon as there is only one cup of your favorite yoghurt on the table for dinner, we are under. The children, no matter how loving and well-bred they were before, know no mercy and struggle without end. And that, although they would probably all ignore the yogurt, there would be five cups of it on the table. Does that sound familiar to you, dear reader? Creating scarcity is a very good way of influencing people. Logically, this only works for my children with yoghurt, chocolate, gummy bears or something like that.

I use the same technique in many places in my program. For example, if I want a task to be done quickly by a contributor on stage, then I'm running out of time. For example, it used to take some viewers a long time to come up with a certain symbol and then paint it on. With the principle of scarcity, I meanwhile get everyone, without exception, to hurry up: I just give them ten seconds and count backwards from ten to zero aloud. That works wonders.

Another example: For a number in my lecture, I need the help of six people from the audience. As soon as I say: "I would like six people up here on the stage", the whole act could possibly burst because nobody wants to go on stage. If I artificially reduce the space on the stage and severely limit the opportunity to participate beforehand, the reaction is completely different. So I say, "There are a thousand people here tonight. Unfortunately, therefore, not all of you have the opportunity to participate personally in this up front. But six of you can be there for my next number. " Since then, more than enough have been available immediately.

The principle of scarcity states that our possibilities appear to us all the more attractive the more difficult they seem to be attainable. A stamp that is only available once is of inestimable value for collectors. This has to do with the fact that it is only through its uniqueness that it achieves its meaning. Paper and printing are no more valuable here than with any other postage stamp. It just has to do with the fact that we make them valuable because of scarcity. And this fact immediately brings me to a realization by Paul Watzlawick: "There are first and second level realities." The fact that the postage stamp is just a piece of printed paper is part of the reality of the first order. The fact that we ascribe an inestimable value to the postage stamp because it is unique is a second-order reality. This distinction is extremely important for any type of communication. Since the world is what we think it is, communication can only function smoothly if the participants in the conversation can sense and accept the reality of the other.

Psychologists have found that this principle works even better when we are reminded that we could irretrievably lose something we already have. In a test, students reacted more strongly to the idea of "loss" than to the idea of making a profit. Psychologists Beth Meyerowitz and Shelly Chaiken, for example, found that cancer prevention brochures are far more effective when women are made aware of what they will lose if they do not go for a check-up than when they emphasize what an early diagnosis would bring benefits. As is so often the case, the change in perspective is decisive here and has a resounding effect.

As soon as we have something that we also have to let go of, it becomes more important. Freedoms once gained are not simply given up. You can make life very difficult for your children and increase the value of the experience if you allow them once to watch TV in the evening and once - for no apparent reason - forbid it. Once there was the freedom to watch television in the evening, it would be a great loss if it were suddenly banned. Please note what I put between dashes above, namely: "for no apparent reason". It follows that it is much easier to maintain a rule if it is not constantly deviated from. Personally, however, I am of the opinion that it can be wonderful for children and parents to enjoy freedoms and thus exceptions together, and that it is ugly to constantly ride around on prohibitions. I myself am also a person with a great urge for freedom. For this reason, I am happy to admit them to my children. If I then take them away from them for a good reason - for example, because everyone has to get up earlier the next morning than usual - then I have to be able to give a well-founded explanation. Most of the time, the children understand that too. What they can never understand, however, is the unpredictability of the parents. And be honest with yourself: as a child, you never could stand that either? If I then take them away from them for a good reason - for example, because everyone has to get up earlier the next morning than usual - then I have to be able to give a well-founded explanation. Most of the time, the children understand that too. What they can never understand, however, is the unpredictability of the parents. And be honest with yourself: as a child, you never could stand that either? If I then take them away from them for a good reason - for example, because everyone has to get up earlier the next morning than usual - then I have to be able to give a well-founded explanation. Most of the time, the children understand that too. What they can never understand, however, is the unpredictability of the parents. And be honest with yourself: as a child, you never could stand that either?

You could test the principle of scarcity at the next opportunity, namely when you have another visitor. Serve biscuits on this occasion, but not a whole bowl full, just a few pieces on a huge plate. Your visitors will probably then perceive them to be of higher quality. At least one study from 1975 suggests this conclusion. Here the participants were given cookies to try in the course of a market analysis. Half were offered ten biscuits in a bowl, the other only two biscuits in the same bowl. The participants who were only offered two biscuits rated them as more expensive and better than the other participants.

Robert B. Cialdini has a very good strategy for dealing with shortages: "Although the short selection of biscuits was rated as significantly more desirable, their taste rating was by no means better than the abundant one. Despite the greater desire that the shortage evoked [...], they didn't taste a bit better than the others. This is an important finding. What excites us so much about scarce goods is not the idea of using them, but the idea of owning them. These two things should not be confused […]. Often, however, our interest in a thing is not based on the fact that we simply want to own it, but on its use value: We want to eat or drink or touch it or listen to it or drive it or use it for other purposes. In such cases, it is important to remember that scarce things just don't taste or work better in the least because of their limited availability, nor do they feel, listen or drive any better. " I hope you will still come to me on stage of your own free will.

The question makes the difference

In the summer of 2002 I was standing with my wife, who was heavily pregnant at the time, at an S-Bahn station in Munich. It was afternoon and we were coming back from town where we had bought some baby clothes for our daughter who was about to be born. We were just in a good mood. We waited longer than usual at the platform. The S-Bahn just didn't come. After about fifteen minutes the announcement came that all further trains would be delayed indefinitely due to personal injury. "Great," I said, "another idiot threw himself in front of the train." Slowly we came under time pressure because we still had an appointment in the evening. We had to go to an event where I was supposed to perform. When the S-Bahn finally came, it was really tight. We had to hurry, to come home first and drive from there to the venue. I still had to put together my props and change. In the end everything worked out. We got there early enough and my performance went well. When I returned to the locker room afterwards, my wife was waiting for me, pale as a sheet. The idiot who threw himself in front of the train was a close friend of our family.

I am telling you this story because this friend was not just any old acquaintance, but because he was one of the people who showed me that you can make a living from giving seminars and lectures. In fact, he was the first to motivate me. That was in the late 1990s. I didn't know the profession of speaker until then. After I finished my studies, we both started a company together.

He was a very good seminar leader, and I still use methods and techniques - both on stage and in my seminars - that he taught me many years ago. His name was Dr. Ingolf Glabbatz, and I like to think back to him.

Often with a mix of feelings of sadness and a little helplessness - he was obviously under much more psychological strain than we had all suspected. I think that without Ingolf it would have taken me a lot longer to realize that I am able to cast a spell over people and bring them something special. It's a shame I could never tell him that personally.

At this point I should definitely mention that he also had a mentor whose name is Andreas Bornhäußer. The methods and techniques that I am introducing to you here come for me largely from a seminar by Dr. Ingolf Glabbatz, but the real creator was

Andreas Bornhäußer. Later, at some point, I also bought his book "Presentainment" and was able to draw a lot from it. Even today I can only warmly recommend it. For me, however, the findings are always shared with Dr. Ingolf Glabbatz stay connected.

One of his favorite phrases was that there are two kinds of people: those who make and those who are made with. It is no easier for the second group than the first - but it is more comfortable. If you would like to belong to the first group, I will give you two of his guiding principles. Here is the first one:

"Those affected always want to be involved"

The chapter on hypnosis has already shown it: It is essential to meet people exactly where they are. Only then can you convince them of your ideas. A good way to find out how - and what - people think is something very simple, but for many a book with seven seals: ask skillfully. Which school lessons do you remember most likely? To those in which a - mostly badly dressed - teacher lectured for hours in front of your class, or to those in which a topic was discussed controversially with the teacher - who was a little more dynamic? I owe most of the knowledge from my school days to the good questions my teachers asked, and at the right time. By the way, the most frequently asked question from my teachers was: «Thorsten, why do you gossip so much? " But only by the way.

By the way, when it comes to questioning techniques, one of my favorite principles applies: Energy follows attention. Here is a really gruesome negative example from Ingolf's seminar. At the end of his product presentation, the seller asks the customer: "Is there anything else that could keep you from accepting my offer?" I think there are really sales seminars in which such stupid questions are recommended, and seminar participants who actually ask such questions. On the principle that energy follows attention, this is pretty much the stupidest question to ask at the end of a sales pitch. Even if the customer were only halfway convinced at this point, this manslaughter question would immediately draw their attention to the negative aspects of the offer. So please delete such questions from your catalog without replacement. We want to deal with four types of questions in this chapter:

- With the leading question: "Was the car red or black?" This question already gives two alternatives. Maybe the car was blue. And: "You are probably already very tired", unfortunately that never works with my children.

- With the final question: You can only answer a decision question with yes or no, possibly with "maybe" or "I don't know". An example: "Do you like this book?"

- With the opening question: It usually starts with a «W». How much, why, why, to what, whom, to whom, by what means? Specifically: "What do you like best about this book?" It has the great advantage of being able to encourage the person asked to speak. When used correctly, it will pique their interest and learn about their attitudes and the way they think. You can of course also specifically influence a decision with the opening question. However, please pay attention to the type of question you are asking for the attention and energy that you get through your question. In the above example - which could still keep the customer from declining the offer - that went completely wrong. Furthermore, you should forget the words "why", "why" and "why" from now on in the opening question. As for these three, we all react biased. We associate an answer with them immediately. Please note: Usually people first say no and then ask "why".

- And finally with the alternative or decision-making question: "Coarse or fine bratwurst?"

Let's take an example from my everyday life: It's seven o'clock in the evening. Time for my children to go to bed. Almost every day one of them comes up with the question: "Dad, can I still eat chocolate?" My answer is usually - except maybe at Christmas: "No." The reaction of my children is the same every time: "Why not?" I am then happy that they start trading with me. It's fun every time. But that's not the point now. Rather, the example is intended to show that the word "why" often occurs with the word "no". Since the energy follows the attention, we do not want to get caught in this suction in the first place. So, forget the why and ask differently - it's far more effective, believe me.

For example, my children could say: "Dearest dad, if I brush my teeth very thoroughly afterwards, then you certainly don't mind that I now eat a little piece of chocolate as a bedtime treat ..." My son actually gave me this print-ready sentence sometimes whispered in the ear in the evening. I was excited! Not only had he turned a question into a statement, he had also turned it into a suggestive statement. Maybe it was all a bit cumbersome, but he's only five years old. Of course he got a piece, so much rhetorical talent has to be rewarded. The example also shows that it can be great fun to follow such a suggestion. Of course I know that my son - boiled down for who he is - tried to influence me.

The leading question and the closing question practically belong in the manipulation training kindergarten. We are now in the third millennium, and many of our fellow human beings have achieved a certain level of education. For this reason, you should recognize these two types of questions as such, but not apply them yourself. Influencing in such a cheap way is too clumsy and lackluster. Only children are allowed to do this. By the way: The over-used management truism "He who asks, leads" is only half the story. It should be more correct: "Anyone who asks, listens and observes well, easily puts the pure questioner in his pocket."

When it comes to alternative questions, Bornhäußer has a very good anecdote in his book: If used correctly, it can lead to a gold mine. He tells of an innkeeper who wants to sell his beef broth with eggs in the future. The innkeeper was enthusiastic about his idea himself, because he calculated that he could achieve a much higher price for his soup with very little additional expenditure. With this goal in mind, he asked his waitresses to offer more broth with eggs in the future. Still nothing changed. The new soup variant did not sell more often than before. Amazed, he told his colleagues about his plan. They were also immediately enthusiastic about the broth-with-egg idea. Why it hadn't sold better than normal beef broth so far was a mystery to them.

They met again two weeks later. The new consommé had become a bestseller for one of the innkeepers. The solution to the resounding success was amazingly simple. True to the motto "The energy follows the attention", this host had benefited from the power of the right question. He instructed his staff to ask the guests the following question: "Would you like the soup with one or two eggs?" Most of the guests replied: "Thank you, with an egg, please."

A very nice addition to the alternative question is the implication. An example of this would be: "Do you clean your shoes before or after lunch?" That is doubly nifty. First, it is assumed that the person being addressed tidies up their shoes at all, and second, two things are linked that have nothing to do with each other. Lunch and tidying up are two different things - please mind the pun. The implication hits the unconscious directly, the conscious is bypassed. By the way, advertising makes masterful use of such implications. Or do you find that deodorant has something to do with seduction? Or vermouth with sex?

Back to the questioning technique. The above example shows the difference between questioning techniques and conducting a conversation. It is not the one who asks, but the one who asks correctly leads: I wrote parts of this book in one of my favorite hotels. This time not in Tuscany or France, but in the Alps in Austria. One evening I ordered a beer with my meal. A light one, to be precise. The waitress gave me a friendly look after the order and asked carefully: "A big one?"

Your follow-up was so friendly that I wouldn't have dared to order a small one - and it was really delicious. That's how you do it. That is pure influence, but a nice one, isn't it? Compare the elegance of this question with a plain and clumsy suggestive question. If the waitress had said: "You want a big beer, don't you?" I would probably have ordered a little water.

Influencing is not a crime. In these cases I don't think they're bad either. Because:

Isn't it the job of a waitress to make the stay as pleasant as possible for the guest, which he still fondly remembers? The waitress helped me make a decision. I had a great evening - maybe because of the great beer - and felt really good. And one more thing: Even though I know the questioning techniques well, I still gladly gave myself up to the seductive influence voluntarily. Effectiveness is the measure of truth that works.

"He who appeals to all the senses makes the most sensible presentation"

That is Ingolf's - or Bornhäuser's - second sentence that I would like to give you here. To show me how we all think on different channels at the same time, he did the following exercise with me. I reproduce them word for word from the seminar documents. You can also find it in the book "Presentainment".

"Imagine wanting to buy a house. You have the following three offers. Please choose one of them. You are about to learn something about yourself:

- «House 1: The house immediately catches the eye with its richly structured facade. You can see at first glance that the owner has devoted his full attention to the design of the courtyard as well as that of the spacious garden. If you look around the five rooms in the living area, you will always discover details that delight the eye. Through the large windows you can enjoy the view of a picturesque part of the city, in which a car is rarely seen. Thanks to the clear architectural design, the living spaces are spacious. It is obvious that this beautiful house is worth the price. "

- «House 2: The second house is extremely attractive. It's in a quiet neighborhood, and the chirping of birds is often the only sound that can be heard here. When the gate opens when you knock and you first step through the secluded courtyard into the garden, you will enjoy the silence. Describing the interior design of the five rooms is almost impossible. It could come from a fairy tale world and tells so much about the history of this house. You may wonder how anyone could match this wealth of objects so harmoniously. Think carefully about how you want to respond to this offer to buy. "

- «House 3: This building is solidly built and spontaneously gives the visitor the feeling of pleasant comfort. With its five rooms, it is spacious enough to give the impression of unrestricted freedom of movement. At the same time, the warmth of the tasteful interior shows a very relaxed cosiness. The building encloses a courtyard, which is characterized by cozy round arches. From there you come into contact with a place that positively affects every visitor. You can certainly feel how important it is to the seller that this house ends up in good hands. ”

Which house you like best says something about how you want to be addressed preferentially. This is because all of the examples are about one and the same house. I had already described the technology of neurolinguistic programming in such detail elsewhere that I could refer to it, but because the method is so fundamental, I would like to come back here shortly afterwards.

In NLP it is assumed that every person perceives their environment via three main channels and communicates via these three main channels: via sight, hearing and feeling. The technical terms are: visual, auditory and kinaesthetic perception. All abilities are present in all people, but they are used differently depending on the person and are not equally pronounced in everyone. The knowledgeable NLP specialist speaks of channel preferences in this context.

There are people who find a message to be presented in an appealing way if it is brought to them visually - for example through photos or films. Others prefer listening to access. They understand a little better when they hear the content and don't necessarily have to acquire it through reading. In turn, others have to literally grasp something, or it has to be addressed for them on the emotional level so that they can remember it well. In this context, it is important to realize that none of us can only be addressed via just one channel. Everyone just has their preferences. They can also change from time to time. So you won't get any further with pigeonholes and generalizations. A person who a few months ago preferred to be addressed via pictures, can now - for whatever reason - suddenly prefer the audio channel. I myself am someone who immediately remembers a text when it is presented to me in a lecture. Once I'm just reading something, I have to focus much more on the content in order to be able to grasp and retain it. It used to be different because I preferred the visual.

In order to be able to assess your counterpart in this regard and to be able to reach them more easily, you have to keep watching them closely. Which aspects you best keep an eye on and which conclusions you can draw from them are detailed in my book "I know what you think".

With the help of the texts that describe the same house in different ways, you can check which channel is currently preferred by you. Suppose you liked house one best. Then your preference is in the visual area. If the second house appealed to you the most, then you currently prefer the auditory channel. Enthusiasm for the supposed third house means: the kinaesthetic channel is currently switched on.

This phenomenon is also one of the reasons why some speakers do better than others with the same content of a speech. If I have a group of people sitting in front of me at a lecture or seminar, then of course I want to reach everyone at the same time: After all, I'm a rampage pig and vain at that. I do this with several tools:

I try to be in the mood from the moment I want to put my audience in: "All power comes from within." I know beforehand what I want to convey to my audience. So I've developed an attitude towards my job. When this point came up at a seminar, some participants smiled and said that this aspect was a matter of course. Unfortunately this is a fallacy. I think Gerhard Polt wrote the following saying: "Because he had nothing to say, he talked for fifty minutes." And that shows exactly what it has to be about.I always try to address all channels in front of a group in order to reach everyone.

Read feelings

Paul Ekman has researched more successfully in this field than almost anyone else. His analyzes were able to show, for example, that our faces invariably show what we feel. Because there is a direct connection between our emotions and our expression. One affects the other. There is no such connection between feelings and our words. Because of this, you can lie with your mouth but not with your face.

Charles Darwin believed that feelings lost their function, their importance, because people developed into higher beings. Today we know that feelings are the basis of all actions. Everything that is important to us is linked to a certain emotion. Every thought, even every rational consideration. That is why those who know how their counterpart is emotionally are able to gain an insight into their innermost being. This can be as convincing as if you could literally read your mind. Recognizing the feelings of others is therefore invaluable.

Unravel emotions and cause a stir

I love faces. Well, it depends on the respective face, but generally I like it and am fascinated by it. By the way, we all are. If you can't believe it, then take a look in your wallet. There are likely to be photos of the people you love there. You can certainly see their faces and not necessarily their feet.

A few years ago I heard a story that illustrates this wonderfully: In England, one of the most famous universities allegedly once had a very prominent professor with a secret quirk. He loved to bathe in the river stark naked. One day he cooled down again and heard a rowboat approaching around the next bend. He thought he recognized two of the rowers' voices. It was probably two of his PhD students, if he wasn't fooled by everything. So he urgently had to come up with something to keep his crazy passion a secret. So he swam as fast as he could to the river bank and tried to hide. Just as he reached the bank, the boat actually turned the corner. His impression was correct the two doctoral students sat in the boat. So he grabbed his towel as fast as he could - and put it over his head! A smart man.

Paul Ekman is one of the pioneers when it comes to researching our facial expressions. After years of studies around the world, the researcher and his team were able to create a face atlas in which he assigned thousands of facial expressions to specific emotions. He developed a system with which one can recognize which emotion is currently being reflected in a face. Maybe you know the series "Lie to me"? The role model for the main character of the series is Paul Ekman. He was also available as a scientific advisor for the implementation. Paul Ekman called his invention FACS, Facial Action Coding System. He had thus developed an ingenious method for deciphering facial expressions. This is based on the fact that there are seven basic emotions that show up in each of us in the same way, as soon as a certain feeling arises in us. They are as follows:

- Surprise,

- Anxiety,

- Sadness, despair,

- Anger and anger

- Disgust,

- Contempt as well

- Joy.

Of course there are far more than these seven different kinds of emotions. But these seven are universal. This means that they are easy to distinguish because they are expressed in the same way in every person.

Paul Ekman researched scientifically, that is, systematically, how each of these emotions is reflected in our faces. This means that if we know his system, then we can read in the face of the other what he is feeling at the moment. That is, to say the least, the Oberhammer. So if you know what to look for in the face of the other person, then you will be able to correctly interpret his emotions. That opens up incredible possibilities for us.

Ekman goes one step further and claims that predictions are even possible. If you have children, you know the situation where you realize that your child is about to start crying. You can see it in the trembling chin and the darkening eye area. This also works for other emotions and for adults. With plenty of practice and a great deal of sensitivity, you can recognize how the other person feels, before the other person realizes it and admits to it. This is what I call high school mind reading. And even if the person you are talking to tries to play something for you, once you know what to look for, you can recognize his true emotion.

According to Paul Ekman, there are several types of facial expression: referential, partial, weak, and micro-expression. The referential facial expression is not very pronounced. It points to an emotion that we don't really feel right now. If someone tells you a story that shows they were upset about something, you may be showing the feeling of anger on your face in order to subconsciously build rapport. So you express anger without feeling it. Ekman explains that it is like saying the word "trouble" with your face. The facial expression is slightly modified so that the other person can see that you support his statement, but you must not inadvertently think that you are actually angry about what has been said. Therefore, only part of the facial expression is used in the referential expression. In trouble like this, you may just pull your eyebrows together or you may press your lips together. As soon as the expression becomes too strong, it is not only irritating for the other person, but there is also the risk that you start to really get angry. After all, the energy follows the attention. Gestures and posture can therefore also trigger the corresponding emotion. After all, the energy follows the attention. Gestures and posture can therefore also trigger the corresponding emotion. After all, the energy follows the attention. Gestures and posture can therefore also trigger the corresponding emotion.

With partial facial expression, only part of the face is involved - in contrast to fully developed facial expressions, the emotion is shown in the entire face. The partial facial expression can have two causes: Either the underlying impulse should not be shown, or it is only weakly pronounced and therefore does not unfold over the whole face.

The weak facial expression is self-explanatory: it is weak. (I love such convincing sentences.) It speaks for a suppressed feeling or for an emotion that is only felt very weakly. It can therefore also be that a conversation partner tries to suppress his emotions, but he does not fully succeed. Even with the slow emergence of a certain feeling, facial expressions only begin to develop weakly, but gradually become more and more clear.

Micro-expression or micro-expression comes about when our emotions briefly

activate special muscles in our face, which we then try to control immediately. Despite the direct control, there is often a facial expression that we control within fractions of a second - the micro-expression.

The micromimic usually extends over the whole face. But that doesn't always have to be the case. There are also moments in which a micro-expression is partially or only very weakly developed. The new printout can then only be seen extremely briefly, about only a fifth of a second. If, as an observer, you blink at that moment, you may not notice it. The microexpression is extremely tell-tale. It usually reveals a feeling that the person concerned is eager to hide. The person you're talking to obviously doesn't want you to know what he's feeling. It can also be an unconscious expression of a feeling. Usually the expression is slightly asymmetrical, it appears and disappears suddenly.

Before we take a closer look at the individual impulses, one thing is crucial: If you want to be able to interpret expressions, you need to know which face your counterpart is showing if it does not show any particular emotion, i.e. if the person is behaving neutrally . As always, calibration must also be carried out here. But now we come to the individual types of emotions and their correspondence in our face.

surprise

That is of course my favorite impulse. My evening programming is designed to create that expression in my viewers, just like joy.

Of all the emotions, the surprise is the shortest. As soon as we know what's going on, we're no longer amazed. As soon as the unexpected has been processed, the expression of surprise changes into another facial expression. The transitions are fluid, by the way. Since it is in the nature of things that a surprise always catches us cold, it is practically impossible to hide it. As long as we do not claim to know exactly about an event beforehand, it is also no problem for our counterpart if surprise shows on our face. In the other cases - where we want to hide our surprise - we are unlucky, because when there is a real surprise we have almost no time to check our behavior.

There are differences of opinion in emotion research as to whether surprise is a real emotion or not. I do not want to leave this discussion unmentioned, but I do not want to go into it further here because it would not help us at this point. Surprise is easy to see in the face, and that alone matters here.

However, it is important to make a distinction between surprise and shock. All researchers agree that it is clearly not an emotion. Being frightened and surprised are reflected in a completely different way on the face. In my seminars, I like to walk slowly through the audience and suddenly yell at someone out of the blue. Yes, my seminars are great fun for those involved. Almost all those affected close their eyes tightly at these moments, lower their eyebrows and tense their lips. If we are surprised, on the other hand, we open our eyes wide, raise our eyebrows, and our famous jaw drops. A facial expression could hardly be more different. In addition, shock is even shorter than surprise, and it cannot possibly be stopped. Even if you tell someone it is about to bang loudly, they will still show signs of fright when they bang - unless they are deaf. This is not the case in

- eyebrows raised high,

- the forehead gets horizontal wrinkles - except in children, adolescents and botox users.

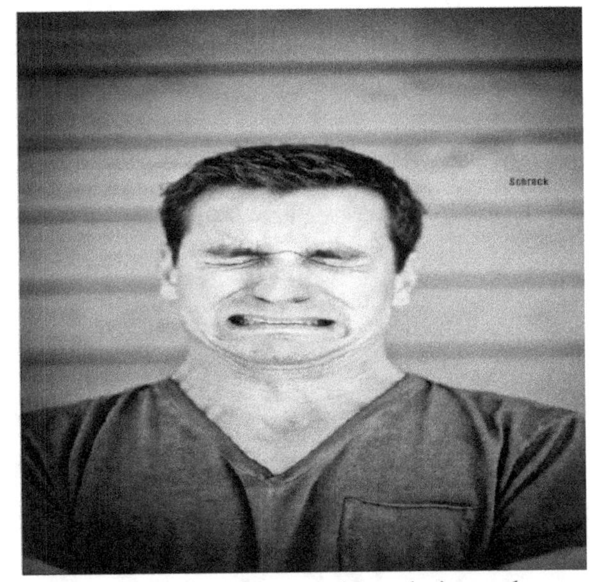

- As soon as a person raises their eyebrows while asking a question, it tells us that they already know the answer. Maybe it's just a rhetorical question. If someone does not know the answer to their own question, it looks very different. In this case, the eyebrows will be drawn together. This expression then does not stand for anger, but for the highest concentration.

- The upper eyelids are pulled upwards, the lower eyelids remain relaxed;

- the lower jaw is down. The further it is folded down, the more amazed it is;

- the expression can be seen briefly. So if you meet someone and they look at you in surprise for more than a few seconds, then either they are not surprised or you confuse the expression with fear.

anxiety

The facial expression in fear is often confused with that in surprise. They are actually very similar. We get scared when we are threatened with harm. The damage can also be psychological. For example a material loss or a physical loss: We have to go to the dentist and we fear pain. There are widespread fears that just thinking about it makes us feel anxious. Snakes and great heights are just two examples that Ekman also cites. Because fears are so easy to evoke, most studies have been conducted on it. It is believed that evolution has two main responses to fear: hide or flee. When we are afraid, our leg muscles immediately receive more blood. The first preparations for the escape are being made.

The other option is to hide. The reaction of becoming rigid with fear and being unable to move has its origins in it. You don't want to be discovered, in other words, you have to hide. It is also possible that we are afraid, but neither the option to flee nor the option to hide is available. If so, it is very likely that fear will turn into anger. Quite often, fear and anger are experienced in rapid succession, according to Ekman. This means that in such cases our nervous system immediately exchanges one emotion for another if the former proves to be ineffective. Signs of fear are expressed in facial expressions as follows:

- Raised eyebrows, but they stay straight.

- Unlike the surprise, the eyebrows are pulled together slightly. The inner ends approach each other.

- The upper eyelids are pulled up.

- When the lower eyelids are tense when the upper eyelids are pulled up and the rest of the face shows no movement, it is never about surprise, but always about fear.

- The lips are tensed horizontally - in the event of a surprise, the mouth is slightly open.

- As soon as only the mouth contorts slightly, but the eyes remain neutral, this is usually a sign of concern.

- The only emotion that leaves the forehead and eyebrows uninvolved is the debilitating form of fear. Only the eyes and mouth change as described above.

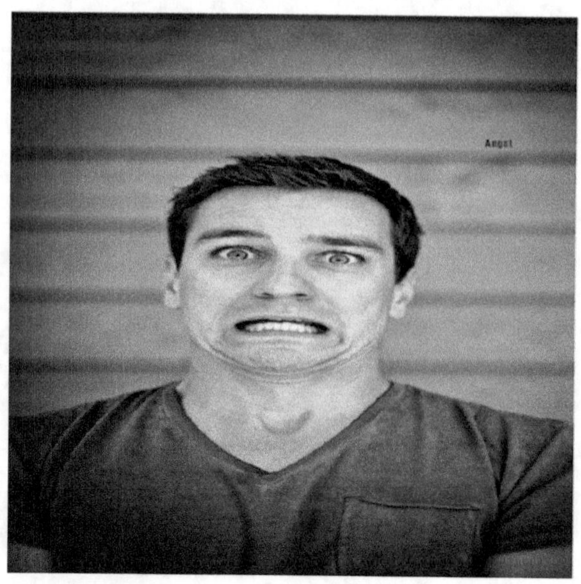

Sadness and despair

As for the length of the expression, the feeling of sadness shows up for a long time - very different from surprise. No emotion is more lingering than grief and despair. In this section, however, I will devote myself exclusively to feelings of depression and despair and not to the extreme expressions of grief, such as those shown by parents at the funeral of their child. Nobody needs a clever book to recognize this level of grief.

No, this is about feeling sad when we haven't achieved something or when a loss is not yet behind us. When we are down, our face is slack and remains without any movement. You can see what is going on by the position of the eyebrows. They will be pulled up on the inside. Because Woody

Allen has eyebrows that naturally point up above the bridge of his nose, he always has a sad face. The actor and comedian Jim Carrey too, by the way. Since only very few people can consciously raise their eyebrows on the inside, this type of facial expression - except for Allen and Carrey - is a very reliable indicator for sadness and despair. Most people create a vertical fold here that betrays these emotions. This position of the eyebrows is sometimes the only sign of sadness. The eyelids are also pulled up by the eyebrows. The inner sides of the upper eyelids get a slightly triangular shape:

When there is great sadness, the lower eyelid is also slightly tense. Another characteristic of grief is the lowered gaze.The corners of the mouth are drawn down.

Anger, anger, anger

Here we have come to the most dangerous of all emotions. Anger is a treacherous

emotion because anger can trigger even

more anger in us. It's a feeling that likes to rock itself up. Furthermore, it is very difficult not to react angrily to someone else's anger. Sometimes you don't even need a second person to get angry. And it can even turn against us. There are moments when you don't like yourself. Usually we get angry when we want to do something and are prevented from doing it. My married readers will certainly know what I mean by this. Even if we are wrongly accused of something, we are insulted or if someone has a completely different opinion, there can be outbursts of anger and anger. In extreme cases, this may lead to that we want to consciously hurt the other, either through words or through physical violence. Anger and anger usually dissipate quickly. However, if the feeling of anger becomes a basic attitude, it becomes dangerous. Rampages, violent attacks against individuals, bloody revolutions are the result. Most of the time, however, the feeling changes into another emotion such as fear.

Anger, anger, and anger are important emotions nonetheless. Without feeling anger, some people would never act and manage to change their situation. Here it is important that we have ourselves under control, that emotions are always directed against the cause and are not transferred to a person who is absolutely unable to help. When we are really angry, we often act rashly and let off steam when we do wrong. You know what I mean by that. In any case, it is more skillful to go into the forest in moments of anger and first yell at a tree, hit a punching bag with all your might or listen to really loud music. When we are in control of the situation again, we can address the cause and have the opportunity to think with a clear head. It's easy to write, I know. For the same reason, it is also not wise to reply immediately to an email that has made us angry and to show the other under power "where the hammer is." It is usually wiser to write an angry reply email and not send it! As soon as we have a cool head again, we simply read our answer in peace and will then be able to assess whether we really want to answer that sharply or not. That is real freedom of thought. we just read our answer calmly and will then be able to assess whether we really want to answer so sharply or not. That is real freedom of thought. we just read our answer calmly and will then be able to assess whether we really want to answer so sharply or not. That is real freedom of thought.

To recognize anger, you need to pay attention to your counterpart's forehead, eyes and mouth. Signs of anger are expressed in facial expressions as follows:

- The eyebrows are lowered and contracted.

- In between, vertical folds usually arise.

- The brow is not furrowed.

If only the eyebrows change, it could be for one of the following reasons: The person

is angry but doesn't want you to see it. She is, however, easily irritated. Or, she may just be amazed and screw up her eyes to focus on the one point that caused the reaction. If eyes or eyebrows are squeezed together, this is usually a clear indication that the person concerned is completely concentrating on the one thing that is fixing them. So if your counterpart does this in a conversation, it can be a very clear indication that they need their full concentration to follow your explanations.

- The upper eyelids are raised with lowered eyebrows, the look is piercing.

- Depending on the severity of the anger, the lower eyelid is tense.

- The upper eyelid lowers at the same time as the eyebrows, which contributes to a gaze that intensely fixes the person opposite.

Danger! If we only consider the eyes, all of the expressions that have been described here so far can also mean that our counterpart is very concentrated. In such cases, the mouth provides information.

- Often the lower jaw - and with it the chin - is pushed forward.

- The lips are tightly closed - you don't say anything more. The red of the lips becomes weaker. If only the lips are pinched together, then that is - be careful - also an indication of concentration or hard physical work. If you pick up something heavy in front of a mirror, you'll know what I'm talking about.

- The mouth is opened in a rectangular shape: after all, there is no point in trying to scream with your mouth closed.

If the other person presses their lips together, this is often a sign that anger is just emerging. This may show you how the other person will react in a moment, even though he or she is not even aware of it. This type of emotion uses muscles that we can control very easily. Because of this, anger is easy to play with. If there is any suspicion, you should at the same time pay attention to the order of his words and the associated actions.

disgust

If you have children, you can regularly see how disgusting looks like: just cook spinach for lunch. If you want to experience for yourself how you feel disgust, then for almost everyone the thought of feces, vomit, urine or green sputum is enough. Again, those with children have an advantage.

Paul Ekman also describes a very vivid thought experiment on the subject of "disgust". It comes from the psychologist Gordon Allport. The idea could also have been from my children.

Disgust experiment

- Swallow the saliva in your mouth.

- Now imagine that you spit a lot of saliva into a glass and then soak it out. Please just imagine that. Something very natural suddenly becomes nauseating. A product that leaves our own body becomes something disgusting from that moment on.

Disgust can be triggered by many factors: by looking at disgusting pictures, by smells, when touching a slimy mass and while watching TV, for example at the "Musikantenstadl" or something like that.

We can be disgusted with other people too. The closer a person is to us, the less often we feel disgust. Because of this, we can change our children's diapers and clean up their vomit without batting an eyelid. For those readers who are about to start a family: this is just the beginning ...

The disgust limit is also shifted during sex. That sounds very unromantic, but it's true. I can therefore bring it closer to you in another way: kissing the lips of a loved one is beautiful, while kissing the lips of someone who repels us is disgusting. We feel differently because of familiarity, closeness, and love. In this context, Ekman also describes that the sight of blood usually repels us. However, our reaction is completely different when the person concerned is not a stranger to us but is close to us. In this case, disgust turns into compassion. We feel the need to alleviate the suffering of the person we love and we do not shrink from anything. Signs of disgust are expressed in facial expressions as follows:

- The nose is always wrinkled.

- The upper lip is pulled up.

- The lower lip can also be pulled up - but does not have to be.

- The lower lip is pushed forward.

- The stronger the disgust, the more wrinkles form around the mouth.

- The eyebrows can be lowered. Warning: There is a risk that disgust will be confused with anger. When the upper eyelids are not raised and the eyebrows are not drawn together, it is often about disgust rather than anger. Most of the time, the muscles around the eyes are relaxed - unless one thing is so gross that we shut our eyes tight because we don't want to see the misery.

Disgust mainly shows around the mouth and nose area. Since we have very good control of the muscles in this area, it is very easy to act disgusted. My kids are great at it, I just have to turn on weird music. It is also easy to hide disgust for the same reason. This only works for me as long as I don't have to lean up any cat shit. Why do they always work on arpets and never on tiles?

Contempt

Recognizing the signal for the reaction "contempt" can save your relationship! Psychologist John Gottman has developed a test that enables him to tell in less than an hour whether a couple's marriage will last or not. Malcolm Gladwell describes in his book

"Blink" how Gottman tells a happy-looking couple after just fifteen minutes of careful observation where the relationship is caught. After only fifteen minutes of analysis, he was able to achieve a hit rate of a respectable ninety percent in this regard. Even after an observation phase of only three minutes, his rate was still close to ninety percent.

His conclusion: As soon as even slight signs of disgust and contempt appear on one of the two partners' faces during a conversation, the relationship is very bad. The rule is that if a couple is not going to get divorced, their positive and negative feelings are at least five to one.

Gottman found that when observing couples, it is sufficient to focus on four aspects: contempt, defensive stance, blockade, and criticism. Gottman calls these four the "apocalyptic horsemen". The worst: contempt. As soon as it shows up on the other person's face during an argument, the couple has a serious problem in their relationship.

Criticism is of course annoying without end, but contempt is far worse because it comes down from above. By despising another person, you are indirectly telling them: You are far below me. Gottman even found that the level of contempt can even be used to predict how often the despised person will catch a cold: As soon as someone I love shows me their contempt, it has such a debilitating effect on my immune system, that I catch cold faster. So much for the clear separation between body and mind.

Contempt and disgust are closely related, but not to be equated. There are important differences when it comes to facial expressions:

- The movement only takes place in one half of the face.

joy

What is characteristic of our society is the fact that research knows so much more about negative feelings than about positive ones. In the past, the majority of scientists were concerned with mental disorders and less with what makes us happy. As the energy follows attention, it is very welcome that this is changing now. It is of great benefit to us to know more about our positive emotions. To find out what triggers it and how we can use it for a happy life. In the following section we will deal with pleasant, positive emotions such as happiness, fun, pleasure - all the exhilarations that we can summarize under the term "joy". Usually we show our happiness to others by laughing or at least smiling. Laughter, on the other hand, can be real with false teeth and false with real teeth. How do you know that?

Well, with a real laugh, your eyes always laugh with you. Ekman has researched how laughing contradicting emotions - like fear or contempt - can sneak in and turn them into a fake laugh. The two muscles that make a laugh "real" and a really happy laugh are also called the "Duchenne markers". Guillaume-Benjamin Duchenne was a French scientist who first examined the differences between real and fake laughter in the 1860s. On the one hand, it was there that he discovered the role of the "zygomaticus major" muscle. He pulls the lips up on the sides to the cheekbones. On the other hand, there is the "orbicularis oculi muscle". This pulls the cheeks up and causes the skin to wrinkle on the sides of the eyes.

Ekman and his colleague Friesen have

researched the topic for decades. Before,

nobody had thought it possible that you

could read hidden feelings in your face. They have now found that the Duchenne markers are just one of several characteristics of a real laugh. For example, the zygomaticus major muscle is activated for a shorter period of time with a real laugh than with a fake one. So a short smile is probably more real than one that is too long.

In the course of these studies, Ekman also found that a real laugh makes people feel even better. So once we are happy we laugh, and when we laugh it makes us happy. Actually, we could all distinguish a real laugh from a fake laugh if we only wanted to. Actually! We don't want that. There is the hypothesis that, for example, we want the lady at the checkout to be happy to

see us. We want other people to smile kindly when we see us, and we act accordingly. It's just nicer than imagining that they don't actually like us or that they even don't care about us. For this reason, we also like to believe a fake smile.

By the way: Most of the time, the facial expression lasts for about two seconds when there is an emotion. Sometimes it only lasts half a second or four. The longer the expression lasts, the stronger the emotion behind it. A reaction that only flashes very briefly usually means that the person concerned wants to hide their feeling, consciously or unconsciously, because they are trying to get their face under control again immediately. If the facial expression lasts longer and is only weakly developed, it is usually a controlled feeling.

The facial expression does not allow any conclusions to be drawn about the cause of the emotion! So we only know what emotion is behind a facial expression. But we never know why this impulse came about and what triggered it. And: Our personal expectations and convictions, whether we want them to or not, always have an impact on how we interpret a facial expression and what we accept as the trigger. So we always have to keep in mind that the facial expression can give us information about the emotion, but does not reveal anything about the objective origin of the emotion.

The truth about the lie

"He said that artists lie to tell the truth. But politicians lie to cover up the truth. " A film quote from «V for Vendetta». After I was able to convict numerous liars on television and have already told all of my best stories in the foreword to Paul Ekman's book "I know that you are lying", I didn't want to write this chapter at first. Until one day I read the reviews of Ekman's book on "Amazon". Among other things, a reader wrote there that the work was far too lengthy for him. In the end he said: "Last note: Maybe JACK CONNOR should give himself a push and at least write a light version of the book." Please, I like to do that. Here is my stripped down version.

In order to expose a lie, one has to pay attention to a great many things in the liar. Even at the risk of repeating myself: The most important thing is to observe the change in the face or body of the person you are talking to, which you have to recognize and keep an eye on. We support what is said through body language and emphasis in our statements. That helps the observer. As soon as the stress or a body expression does not match a statement, we can assume that the words are not meant as they were uttered. In our technological world, it is becoming more and more difficult to evaluate the emphasis or facial expressions behind a statement.

That is not entirely unproblematic. Because we feel this, we resort to tools that, in my opinion, have infected the written word like a virus - I'm talking about emoticons. This term is made up of emotion and icon and is a symbol that makes the feelings and intentions of the text author clear. Let's say someone text you a cold joke. The sender might think: "Hm, maybe the recipient won't be able to tell on his own that I'm trying to make a joke - I just add a colon, a dash and a parenthesis. » Almost all mobile phones are now programmed to recognize this character string and to insert a smiley on their own, as soon as you type the colon and the dash. If the ghastly emoticons are not enough for you, you can go one step further. At the end of his messages he just puts a few letters that stand for certain idioms in cyber society: for example LOL or - the height of stupidity - ROFL. This is English. It must be good with that. The fact that half of Germans don't know what that really means doesn't matter at all. That's not really a shame either, it's pretty nonsense anyway. LOL means "laughing out loud", which means something like "I start laughing out loud", and ROFL means "rolling on the floor laughing" or "rolling myself with laughter". What is happening here with our language? Not only that we don't use ours, but another, no, we also mess up another language that most of us only half understand. Feel free to think of me as old-fashioned about this - so am I. I'm an analog guy in a digital world. Incidentally, this sentence is not mine. It's from Hank Moody, one of my favorite authors.

I am always asked whether I have any tics - here comes one: I detest English terms in the German language: There is no more coffee to take away - unfortunately it is over, there is only coffee to go, meetings, wedding Planner, approaches, managers, awards, background, back-ups, backstage, basics, benchmarks, bikes, blackouts, bodyguards, body lotions, boots, brainstorming sessions, breaks, business-to-business, business-to-consumer, call centers, canceled shows , Catering services, charts, city centers, check-ins, Xmas, coaches, comedy and so on and so forth. And these are just the superfluous terms in my opinion up to the letter C. One could fill entire volumes with such words alone.

But it gets the craziest from the moment we seem to use English terms in German, even though they don't exist in English at all. Neither the Americans nor the English know a cell phone, and a callboy is not the same in English as it is in German - in the USA it is a page, nothing else. (If you don't know what a callboy is in German, I envy your unspoiled nature.) The problem with these mindless language frauds is not just that our language is messed up with it - no, it even goes as far as English Advertising slogans (sorry, "slogans") such as "Come in and find out" or "Have a break, have a kitkat" are what most Germans only understand Railway Station. According to an article on Spiegel online, anglicisms are not a good choice in advertising.

To test how they were received by consumers, 24 test subjects were connected to a lie detector. Then their skin resistance was measured when playing the German and English advertising messages. Conclusion: "Are you still living or are you already alive?" and "I love it" works better than "Come in and find out" or "There's no better way to fly". The English advertising messages rolled off the German participants like an egg on a Teflon pan. The contents were not properly understood, nor did they attract the desired attention. "Come in and find out" was nonsensically translated as "Come in and find out".

And I would not like to withhold two wonderful examples on the subject of "Denglish nonsense" from you, dear reader, at this point.

First of all, the word "public viewing". We believe that if we want to describe the fact of how we watch a soccer game with many other people in a public square, then a good English term for it would be "public viewing". Public viewing is about as close to English and American usage as Michael Schumacher is to the next world championship title. In the US, the term means what we would call an inquest. So if you have an English business partner as a guest and ask him if you want to come to the public viewing in the evening, then he thinks there has been a death in your family, is disturbed that you are inviting him of all people and does not leave from that you want to watch football with him.

Another of my favorite examples was reported to me by one of my seminar participants and comes from Lufthansa. A few years ago, the company offered its passengers sealable plastic bags for storing shampoo, toothpaste and other liquids. Wrapped in this way, it was allowed to take them on board in hand luggage. So far, so good, but one nice detail is still missing: the airline had these bags printed with the label "Body bag" - after all, you can take them on the plane in hand luggage or directly on your body. In my opinion, however, the fact that body bag means "body bag" in German is very problematic. You are afraid of flying anyway, and body bags are handed out before take-off.

There is also no longer a good German late breakfast, people only meet for brunch on Sundays. If there is a combination of breakfast and lunch, why do we still meet for coffee and cake and not for a drink or a liner?

By the way, the author Hank Moody doesn't really exist - he is the main character in the series "Californication". If you really want to see an unusual series, then you should definitely check it out. The first scene alone is overwhelming - as long as you can handle swine jokes and tough dialogues. Moody is a writer's block writer living in Los Angeles. In a radio interview, he is asked what is upsetting him. He replies in a general manner that he is incredibly insane, that people are obviously getting more and more stupid. This is normal, by the way, and it will probably happen to us older people sooner or later. Even in his day Goethe was upset about his youth.

Warning: Now it's getting really vulgar - if you can't take it so well, skip the next paragraph! "You know, we have this very unbelievable technology - nevertheless, computers have meanwhile turned into jerking machines for entering four-digit letter codes. The internet should free us, bring democracy. But in reality, it has given us 24/7 access to child pornography. People no longer write, they just blog. Instead of talking, they text. No more punctuation, no grammar. LOL this, LMAO (Laughing My Ass Of - very carefully translated: I'm laughing at myself) that. You know, it seems to me like a group of stupid people with another group of stupid people in a native language 'pseudo ›Communicate that is more like what cavemen have uttered than more appropriate contemporary language." Now,

Back to recognizing lies. Many of us have forgotten how to really notice each other when we are talking. We simply rely on a non-specific feeling that we call gut feeling, but which threatens to wither due to our increasingly technology-dominated world.

Note, by the way, that telling falsehood doesn't always have to be a lie. It is possible that a person actually thinks he is speaking the truth and still says something that we would take to be untruth. This is because there is not just one objectively measurable truth, but at least as many truths as there are people in the world. After all, the principle still applies: "The world is what we take it to be."

Let me illustrate this with an event that kept the whole of Germany in suspense for days: Did Jay Kahn want to make a secret agreement with Sarah Knappik before he started in the jungle camp or not? Sure, in Egypt and Tunisia the world was literally unhinged these days, but the majority of Germans found the events in the jungle camp more exciting. Well, it was interesting too. At some point, Sarah cleared the table and told everyone in attendance as well as the viewers at home that Jay - who really didn't like her very much - had met with her before the show to make an arrangement with her. They would fake a love affair in front of the world at the camp in order to gain popularity. That confession went off like a bomb. Jay denied this a little too violently for my purposes. Such an arrangement never went and Sarah's claim was - attention, nice German term - bullshit, so Jay.

I'm really sorry that this chapter is so vulgar, I can't help it, I'm just quoting. The next day, the phones at my agency were hot. All private broadcasters as well as numerous tabloid magazines wanted to get my assessment. Was Jay lying - or was Sarah? My assessment: Jay didn't tell the truth, but he didn't lie either. There were clear signs of fear and contempt on his face. However, one must not commit the so-called Othello fault here. That consists in interpreting the fear in the eyes of another person as an admission of guilt. In this case, as an indication of a lie. Fear can also arise from feeling falsely accused. Incidentally, that was the case with Othello's wife. Read it from William

Shakespeare. Hence the name othello bug. Read about it at Ekman. I interpreted the situation as follows: Sarah Knappik was not lying. Jay wasn't lying either, but he wasn't telling the truth either. He might even have met Sarah before the show, hence the horror on his face. However, such a date wouldn't have been a big deal for Jay. That's how it works in show business. Hence no sign of repentance or any other indication of a lie. That's how it works in show business. Hence no sign of repentance or any other indication of a lie. That's how it works in show business. Hence no sign of repentance or any other indication of a lie.

The signals when lying are always that the behavior of the alleged liar suddenly changes in some way. A reliable sign is always a movement or a gesture that could not be observed before. If the person you are talking to suddenly covers his mouth with his hand - or even just one corner of his mouth - that can be a clear indicator of lying. But it may also happen that he wants to express skepticism - or has to vomit right away. To find out, you need more indicators and a lot of intuition. In total, we have three levels at which we can expose a lie:

- non-verbal communication such as gestures, facial expressions, language,

- what words are used, what is the emphasis,

- physical cues such as a change in pulse rate or sweaty palms.

Let us first deal with body language and facial expressions. The signals I am presenting to you here are universal in terms of their meaning. This means that they are largely independent of the respective culture, regardless of whether you see these signals in a person in Timbuktu or Schmelz-Außen, the emotion behind them is likely to be always the same. In addition, when we are under pressure, it is very difficult for us to react differently than described here. This is also one of the reasons why poker players in particular deal very closely with exactly these signals. The name for such treacherous gestures also comes from poker jargon. They are called - also in German - Tell. So this is a gesture that reveals something else, something hidden about us. After reading many lines in this chapter, in order to blaspheme about English terms in the German language, I will continue to refer to the tells here as treacherous gestures. But you should know what a tell is.

These gestures can of course have different meanings depending on the situation and context. In case you are wondering why a person shows a certain facial expression or makes a special gesture in a certain situation, and if you simply cannot assign its meaning, I have a good trick for you: Just imagine that you were doing this gesture do it yourself. How does that feel? It's even easier in front of the TV. Just imitate the facial expression or gesture shown on TV. Since the energy follows the attention in both directions, your emotion not only determines your body language, it also works the other way round. So you always have your translator with you. Don't underestimate this trick. He has already done me the best possible service on stage.

Suppose the person you are talking to starts by pressing their fingertips together and setting up their fingers like a roof while they talk to you or listen to you. At this moment he is probably reflecting on what you are saying or thinking about what to say to it. This gesture is also called the «church tower». If you want to be perceived as thoughtful and independent thinking, you can use this gesture to create exactly that impression. However, caution is advised: too much self-confidence can quickly come across as arrogant.

The following scene happens regularly at home: My son comes home, throws off his jacket and shoes where he is standing and runs into his room. If I then follow him and politely point out that he should please hang up his jacket and put his shoes in the cloakroom, the reaction is usually the same. He looks at me as if I came from another universe, raises both hands, positions them to the side of his head and says: "I always have to do something!" He makes a chopping downward movement with both hands at the same time. Both hands hit the edge of the hand, so to speak, in the air that every karate master would be proud of. He makes it so energetic that you get the impression that he could easily break through blocks of stone that are centimeter thick. If he were to use this energy to hang up and put away, everything would be fine. But it seems to him to be used more sensibly. This gesture is also one of the universal ones. Anyone of us who want to emphasize something very strongly uses our hands in exactly the same way. If someone is not being sincere, it may well be that they are too supportive of a banal statement with this very gesture. This gesture only comes when we really stand behind what has been said with full energy and when what has been said has special weight. In eight and fifteen situations, we tend not to use these. So if it is used here it could be tell-tale. who wants to underline something very strongly uses his hands in exactly the same way. If someone is not being sincere, it may well be that they are too supportive of a banal statement with this very gesture. This gesture only comes when we really stand behind what has been said with full energy and when what has been said has special weight. In eight and fifteen situations, we tend not to use these. So if it is used here it could be tell-tale. who wants to underline something very strongly uses his hands in exactly the same way. If someone is not being sincere, it may well be that they are too supportive of a banal statement with this very gesture. This gesture only comes when we really stand behind what has been said with full energy and when what has been said has special weight. In eight and fifteen situations, we tend not to use these. So if it is used here it could be tell-tale. In eight and fifteen situations, we tend not to use these. So if it is used here it could be tell-tale. In eight and fifteen situations, we tend not to use these. So if it is used here it could be tell-tale.

There is one other movement that we like to use to support the truth of a statement. If we want to emphasize something very much, we move a hand downwards rhythmically when we are making our statement. Most of the time, it is open and the palm of the hand points down when you move it. The whole thing looks like we're about to hit an imaginary table top. This movement has a very dominant effect, we push our counterpart down with it, try to make it small and thus make us bigger. That doesn't necessarily make him feel comfortable.

In men, it is worth taking a look at the larynx. As soon as the muscles make a swallowing movement after a statement - or while listening - this is a good indicator of stress, fear or rejection of what has just been said. So: "I am very happy to see you" - and then a sip follows. Probably not a real enthusiasm.

And then there is the blink of an eye. We usually blink every twenty seconds. In a normal conversation where the person you are speaking to is on the same wavelength as you are, they will blink about as often as you do. Mostly the moment you pause while talking. Anything beyond that could mean that the other person feels guilty, is afraid, is shy - or that their contact lens has slipped. When we think hard, for example to come up with a good lie, the blink rate usually increases. This often goes parallel to the gaze and the line of sight. If you look down, this is usually a good indicator of feelings of guilt. But the same can also be the case if someone has just looked you in the eye for too long and too long. (I have already said You also need your intuition.) In this case it may be that he is trying to hide his feelings of guilt by looking you straight in the eye. It then quickly has something of the who-looks-away-game from school days.

The concentrated look into the eyes can quickly cause stress to arise in our counterpart. Try that with your children. Say, "I can see whether you are telling me the truth or not," and look your child in the eye for a long time without a word. As soon as eye contact is broken, it immediately reduces the stress a little. People who want to appear dominant hold their gaze much longer than those who want to subordinate themselves. Caution: It is therefore possible that your counterpart breaks off eye contact precisely for this reason. He doesn't want to put himself above you or he just likes you. This is the exact opposite of what is commonly thought of long eye contact!

I perform a lie test in my evening program. In most cases, at some point the very ones who are telling the truth avoid my gaze. This little game of who can hold their eyes longer is too stupid for them at some point. After all, they are telling the truth. The liars don't do that. They last forever. They think: "If I look the other way now, that is a sign of weakness. But I mustn't show any weakness, otherwise you can see that I'm lying. " Exactly the opposite is the case.

With this knowledge, I was able to convict a contributor during a shoot for the RTL magazine "Extra". When I asked her what she thought I was watching at the moment of the lie, she meant the fact that she probably couldn't have made eye contact when she lied. In reality, she'd only kept eye contact while lying. For all of the truthful answers, her eyes had always moved in different directions while searching for the correct answer.

Speaking of which, many journalists who had read my first book later asked me if someone would lie if they looked up left before answering. Because according to the NLP theory, this movement suggests a constructed idea. This is of course much too simplistic and can easily be misleading. That's not what it is about. It is always about whether - as in the above example - anything has changed compared to other statements and at what moment this happened.

Ask someone a question and if they touch the back of their head with the palm of their hand while answering, that is a clear indication of uncertainty. If his answer sounds too confident and he emphasizes what he is saying too much, it can show that something is making him insecure. Don't forget: It is precisely this gesture that good manipulators can use to weaken a harsh statement.

Instead of the back of the head, the ears, the side neck or the cheeks can also be touched. In women, the hand wanders to the cleavage more often, a grip here or the chain shows exactly the same thing. The degree of guilt or stress felt can be read from the strength with which the hand exerts pressure on the skin or the object. In general, by the way, we always touch each other particularly often when we want to reassure ourselves. Scratching, rubbing, caressing yourself, kneading your hands or wrists show insecurity, fear, aversion or resistance, depending on the situation. It is important to decide, depending on the situation, Because a light rubbing of the hands or the wrists combined with a very self-confident facial expression can mean exactly the opposite - arrogance or the will to be brutal can be involved. So, if you want to build rapport with someone, it's best to leave out these gestures.

Touching the nose is also such a gesture to leave out. It is always a sign of uncertainty. Bill Clinton touched his nose significantly often during the surveys on the "Monicagate" affair. This was one of the reasons why he looked so insecure. The other reason is that he lied. The grip to his nose was so noticeable that Bill Clinton's media adviser urged him to stop. Opinion polls revealed that it was precisely because of this that he had lost the trust of his constituents.

If someone prefers not to say something, they may press their lips together. That can only happen very easily and hardly noticeably. The clenching of the lips can happen before or after the statement that makes us uncomfortable.

Touching the lips - with your fingers or an object - can reveal a whole range of emotions. In order to interpret these correctly, you should always pay attention to other indicators. It can be a sign of insecurity, stress, fear, or great thoughtfulness. The gesture is also very close to sucking the thumb - that is, a gesture of calming yourself down. If you are talking to someone and they suddenly touch their lips, it may be that it is a sign that they are not speaking their mind. When flirting, touching your lips - or even better, wetting your lips with your tongue - is a sign that you would like to get down to business.

So far we have only dealt with emotional processes while lying. A lie is usually based on emotions such as fear or excitement. Often there is a combination of several of these emotions behind it. Maybe the liar feels guilty. He may fear the negative consequences of his actions, especially if something is really at stake for him. It can also be that he knows that everyone in the room knows the truth and is having great fun behind the interrogator's back at the strict lie. In this case, the liar mostly does not suppress his fear, but rather excitement or a laugh.

In addition to the emotional aspects, there are also the content-related processes that need to be taken into account. Lying is a very complex task. It is exhausting. That is why it is so difficult to lie credibly, especially when we are asked over and over again. Especially if the questioner surprises us, we can easily get into a tailspin. We have to think logically and quickly as soon as we cheat. We may well change our behavior in the process. It's about these changes, they can give us good clues.

By the way, this is one of my favorite ways to quickly spot a story of lies. Let A biz Z tell you a story. Just listen. The longer the other person speaks, the better. When it is finished, simply ask the other person to tell everything again in reverse order, i.e.

backwards. With a lie it will not work conclusively, with the truth it will. Unless they are master liars. The trick is really good. We are so busy making up a lie that we usually cannot keep track of the exact chronological order of events. Therefore, most of the time we cannot tell a story of lies from the back to the front.

The third notable aspect is the control processes. We try to control our behavior in particular and to appear very confident because in reality we are insecure. However, it is precisely this uncertainty that usually flashes through briefly and can, under certain circumstances, be easily recognized by a concentrated observer. The compulsive controlling of the situation seems to be relaxed and it is.

I cannot emphasize it enough: before you start looking for signs of a lie, you first need to know how your interlocutor usually behaves. This is called calibrating. Talk to him about normal things. About topics that are not particularly relevant to you. Observe here whether it shows any tick. Does he rock the chair back and forth, does he play with his ring or his hands? In such a case, the fact that he stops doing it may mean something is wrong. You have now grasped the normal state and a basis on which you can determine changes. So instead of looking for very special gestures, i.e. tells, just observe the overall picture of your counterpart. Once you are just looking for single gestures, you care too much. You are so focused on something that you quickly miss other signals, perhaps very important ones. You miss finding because of searching. Remember: the energy follows attention. Your own attitude in particular determines how much your counterpart shows signs of nervousness or not. Here too, a sure instinct is required. As soon as you act strangely yourself, the other person will do the same. Not because it's lying, but because your strange behavior is affecting its behavior. how much your counterpart shows signs of nervousness or not. Here too, a sure instinct is required. As soon as you act strangely yourself, the other person will do the same. Not because it's lying, but because your strange behavior is affecting its behavior. how much your counterpart shows signs of nervousness or not. Here too, a sure instinct is required. As soon as you act strangely yourself, the other person will do the same. Not because it's lying, but because your strange behavior is affecting its behavior.

Lie to the detector

Unmasking is not achieved in the polygraph test - often incorrectly called the lie detector test - in any other way than described above. First control questions are asked and calibration is carried out. Skin resistance, breathing rate, breathing depth and pulse are measured. Polygraphs are anything but reliable and are therefore not admitted to court in Germany. That's how it should be. In the USA, entire existences have been destroyed due to incorrect polygraph analyzes. But there are also some criminals walking around free because they were able to outsmart a polygraph. I myself once witnessed how it works while filming for the program "Galileo".

You can lie to a polygraph by checking your sphincter. Tense him up when you tell the truth and relax when you lie. It's that simple. But only if the person who operates it lives behind the moon. In the meantime, a pillow is pushed under the buttocks that checks the activity of the sphincter. Yes, there is something like that, you can't even hold back your chair in peace during the interview.

However, one woman had an even better trick at hand when filming "Galileo". Every time she told the truth, she thought of her unpleasant images. She imagined sitting in a burning house or in a car accident. When she lied, she thought of something nice: a day at the beach on vacation or good sex. The more emotional the visualization, the less useful the result was for the operator of the polygraph.

In addition, it has meanwhile been shown in some studies that the operator of the polygraph has to be impartial in order to interpret the data correctly. As soon as he himself has a certain suspicion, the furnace is over, the objectivity is gone. Derren

Brown gives a fine example of this in his book "Tricks of the Mind". In a covert test, scientists had four "experts" carried out interviews with the help of a lie detector. They were supposed to find out which of the four employees had stolen a video camera. However, each of the experts was told in advance which of the men was particularly suspicious. Each was named a different one. The study's researchers wanted to find out whether this information would affect the test results. In reality, no camera was stolen, and all four interviewees were telling the truth. Nevertheless, after the questioning, every expert found his "suspect" guilty.

A polygraph is also just a machine and does not recognize a lie, only differences in breathing, pulse and skin resistance. The values will later be analyzed by a specialist. This means that the device can only ever be as good as the person evaluating the data. With a lot of practice a person can surpass the evaluation of the polygraph. But here too, caution is advised. As soon as the observer is no longer unbiased or stressed or simply overlooks a signal, it no longer works. That is also one of the reasons why I only show such tests because of their entertainment value. In the real world, we all make mistakes.

Paul Ekman was able to show in several experiments that participants in his training - he calls it FACS training, i.e. facial action coding system training - were able to discover eighty percent of the lies. That's a very good rate. In other words, twenty percent of the lies go undetected even with our methods today. If someone has structured the lying well enough, they are unlikely to be exposed. After all, he has told the wrong story so often that in the end he believes in it himself. Then there are talented liars who are just good at it. And finally there are the psychopaths, even Ekman grabs his teeth at them. With them it is impossible to expose a lie.

The stuff that lies are made of

Incidentally, it is not only worth taking a closer look, but also listening carefully. Here are a few things to look out for:

- Pitch. As soon as we are stressed, we speak faster and in a higher voice. If someone asks a question in a higher pitch than the one who is speaking, this is an indicator of genuine interest. Incidentally, the voice is matched to the highest ranking. For example, men in a female-dominated group speak in a slightly higher pitch in order to appear less aggressive and to integrate better into the group.

An alignment to a higher rank has also been observed in the case of the television legend Larry King. If he had guests of a higher status on his show - for example the US President or world stars like Mick Jagger - then he obviously adapted his body language and tone of voice to these guests.

If he ranked his social status above that of his guests, then they were forced to adapt their voice and body language to his. And they did too. Is not this great?

- Less details. When we lie, we are less specific. We are less fond of detail in our descriptions. Details are often left out or only briefly addressed. If you ask a liar for details, he'll probably try to repeat just that, just adding a little more flair to what he's told you before. Much like my youngest daughter after peeing while playing. I noticed it and said to her: «Your pants are all wet. Did you accidentally peed in there? " Her short and very concise answer: "It wasn't me, it was grandma!" I was very concerned about it. At the time she was barely two years old and was already lying without blinking an eyelid. If the story had made sense in terms of content,

- The ego. Lies are less self-centered. That is, the liar uses fewer pronouns like me, mine, me and others more. Rather impersonal expressions and generalizations are used: "as you know", "all", "nobody" and "always". This indirectly creates a distance between the story served and the person.

- Speed. Because the liar has to think while lying and remember many things at the same time, he often speaks more slowly than usual. This is because he can only think one thought at a time. Because of this, he may make promises more often than usual, and the way he speaks may seem very formal. Parasite or delay sounds such as Uh or Hm may increase.

All of the parameters presented here are of course only auxiliary. You just have to consider: good liars may not change their behavior at all or hardly noticeably. Different people also lie differently. There are no one hundred percent reliable signals that lead to the detection of a lie. Even interrogators aren't much better than students at exposing a liar. You can't do it if he's clever and practiced. Specialists usually just have more self-confidence, and that helps them. In most cases, they might as well flip a coin. Your hit rate is fifty-five percent. Not higher!

Nevertheless, it is fun to practice exposing lies and to train one's knowledge of human nature. Don't get discouraged if it doesn't work right away. Every beginning is difficult. Once you are certain that you have seen a significant change, you could try the following strategy: change the subject and talk about something neutral. See if the changes can now be observed again. Then suddenly you go back to the hot topic and see if you can observe something unusual again. The same signals do not have to be set again now. It just depends on whether you discover something that is different from normal behavior. So you know whether the changed signals are really changes in behavior that are authentic, or whether it is a change, which is solely due to any external circumstances. The old sitting position had become uncomfortable, the temperature in the room has changed - whatever the cause.

Finally, I would like to give you my personal favorite tip on the way. He has done me outstanding service with my children. Sometime a few years ago I told my eldest daughter that I could see very clearly from her face - and also from the face of her siblings - if she was lying to me. That wasn't really a lie, in most cases I see it right away with her. Curious what she is like, of course she asked me how I could tell. Now I lied to her and said, "I can see it on the tip of your nose. It will be known every time you lie to me. " These words had a magical effect on my children. Since then, every time they fool, you hold your nose and when they tell the truth, emphasize it bluntly with the words: "That's true. Or is my nose turning white? " Wonderful.

Where is the coin

You can use this number to drive those around you crazy. It consists in the fact that you can repeatedly tell the other person in which hand they are holding a coin.

I offer you two options for this. The first is not one hundred percent reliable, but you can repeat the effect as often as you want, provided it works. You cannot repeat the second method too often, but it is almost a hundred percent safe.

- First option: ask your partner to hide a coin in one hand behind their back. Tell him that in this case you need his cooperation and that he therefore cannot put the coin behind his back in his pocket. Believe me, if you don't say this, it keeps happening. Be that as it may, you must not know which hand he is holding the coin in. Then he should come forward with both hands clenched in a fist.

Even if you have to guess, you still have a fifty percent chance. But we don't want to take advantage of the probability. We don't want to guess which hand the coin is in, we want to know. To find out, don't look your teammate in the eye - as one might suspect - but at the tip of your nose! No matter where the eyes look, the tip of the nose almost always points imperceptibly towards the hand in which the coin is located. I think that's because we unconsciously want to look at the "hot" hand, but don't want to give ourselves away with our eyes. The face - and with it the nose - therefore mostly points in the direction of the hand with the coin. Since the other person does not know that the tip of the nose is pointing at the coin, you can use this tell again and again,

- Second option: If it doesn't work as described above, I have a second, very reliable method. Give your teammate a coin again. Now tell him you're about to turn around. As soon as you have your back to him, he should decide which hand to put the coin in. With this hand he should now grab his forehead and think intensely about the coin and the hand. After about ten seconds of intense thinking, have him hold out both hands and tell you that you can turn around again. If you turn around, you will see a person with two arms outstretched in front of you. You can now tell him repeatably and with almost 100% certainty which hand the coin is in. To do this, just pay attention to the back of his hand. The hand that he held on his forehead for ten seconds will be more bloodless and therefore lighter, that is, less pink or red. Compared to the other hand, which he held down, the veins do not protrude as much.

The nice thing about the number is that you can actually tell from these signs which hand the coin is in. It's just completely different characteristics that are important than your viewer thinks. This trick uses everything that I have written in the chapter about reading faces and recognizing lies: you are watching closely. You calibrate by looking at what color your hand was previously; you concentrate fully on the person opposite you.

By the way, there is one condition under which the number does not work: cold. A few years ago I shot a report with Ingo Nommsen for ZDF. In the sequence I was supposed to first find a pin that was hidden in the Botanical Garden in Munich. Then I was supposed to show the moderator a trick that he wanted to use himself later. I decided on the number just explained. What I hadn't considered: it was winter. Almost everyone wore gloves or had hands so cold that the backs of the hands were bright red anyway. This tip therefore went completely wrong.

Magic of words

"Just words in - or also: with what exactly he." A funny sentence is what is the word salad supposed to mean? Quite simply, at this point my only concern is to show you how we can change meanings by twisting words. Suddenly there is a new perspective. This doesn't really change the sentence, it just signals something completely different. That's exactly what I'm doing now. With a little twist I get to the «magic of words». There is no need to add or remove a letter in the heading. Simply repositioning is enough and the meaning is different. The world is what we think it is.

Language creates consciousness, it is the clothing of our thoughts, and ultimately it makes people. This finding is far from new. In George Orwell's novel "1984", for example, the political caste prescribes an official language. The state determines what should be thought here. This is language education from above par excellence. And by the way, it takes place everywhere in a certain way. For terms such as "people with a migration background", "trainees" and "colored people". These are such cases.

Language creates awareness, makes opinions. Surveys in various countries showed this. Here, citizens were asked in a study, for example, to describe the characteristics of a table. It was not about a specific table, but simply about the object itself. The astonishing result: those in whose language the word "table" had a masculine article - like us Germans - attributed mainly masculine characteristics to the matter, such as "robust". The French, on the other hand, associated it with more feminine attributes, according to the article.

Since I have studied language and live from entertaining and inspiring people with words, it is very important to me. I was particularly impressed by the change of perspective that can be controlled with it.

This also makes it possible, for example, to recognize the true value of something.

A story that shows this very nicely is the following: On a remote island in the South Sea, a pupil listened attentively to the story of the teacher, who was just explaining: "The gifts we give each other are supposed to remind us of love. With gifts, people show that they love each other. " The next day the boy gave his teacher a shell of exquisite beauty. She had never seen anything more beautiful before. "Where did you find this beautiful and precious shell?" She asked her student. The boy explained that there was only one place on the other side of the island where one could occasionally find such a shell. This hidden little bay can be found about twenty kilometers away. "It's just lovely," said the teacher. «I will keep it all my life and therefore never forget you. But you shouldn't have run this far just to give me a present. " With shining eyes, the boy said: "The long way is part of the gift."

Isn't the story of an unknown author touchingly beautiful? After I told about it in a seminar, one of the participants said: "What you get in life is always as valuable as the sacrifice you have made for it." That's the way it is. The watch we get when we graduate from high school may be cheaper than the one we can afford later, but it is still more valuable.

Change of perspective makes you cool

When I walk into the bathroom in the evening and find a messy sink with Lillifee and Käpt'n Sharky toothpaste leftovers including a smeared mirror - and I found it like that every evening for a while - it can annoy me. Today it rarely occurs. Not being smeared, but being angry. Today I think to myself: "Cool, the children thought about brushing their teeth on their own." So my life is much more pleasant. Can you think of any examples from your life in which this way of thinking could help you? However, in rare cases it can also be right not to change your perspective. Namely when you are extremely satisfied and happy. Of course you have to recognize that at this moment ...

A manager came to a large lake on his fishing vacation. An Indian sat there fishing.

"What are you doing?" He asked. "Well, I'm sitting here fishing," was his reply. "If you used two rods, you could catch more fish." - "Why should I do that?" - "Then you would have more money and could soon buy yourself a boat." - "And then?" - "Then you could hire someone to help you and you would earn even more money." - "And then?" - "Then one day you could even have a fish factory and make a lot of money." - "And why should I do that again?" - "Then you could take a leisurely look out over the lake and fish." - "But I'm already doing that," said the Indian.

That's it

We have learned about many methods of influencing in this book. As with everything, it depends on what you make of it. Sure, you can of course use them to win others over and only think about your advantages. This would have failed this book, because that's not what I was after when I wrote it.

Personally, I find manipulation repulsive the moment it is used as a weapon in everyday life. From then on we descend as "manipulators" to the level of windy business people, coffee trip sellers and self-proclaimed heralds of salvation. What you personally do with these methods, you have to decide very subjectively. During my lectures - and also while writing this book - one thing became clear to me again: In private as well as in business it is about more than the pure possibility of influencing. It's about trust, curiosity, passion, closeness. It's about all the things that make our hearts dance when we see happy, laughing children. It's not about fear!

I believe - and this is my very personal opinion - that all control freaks act precisely out of this fear. They are afraid of their own strength, they are afraid of being hurt if they do not achieve their goal. If someone like that arrives at his goal, he has only reached the goal, so he is still a long way from winning. At that moment, something very essential is missing: fulfillment. If all power comes from within, then success without fulfillment is not success.

How can we manage to protect ourselves from these methods so that they do not become a weapon against us? I am asked this question regularly. Well, first of all, of course, it helps to know what means of influencing there are and how these methods can be used. Only with this knowledge can you freely decide whether you want to get involved or not. A second essential factor is strength - and it always comes from within!

Only you have the power to create your own experience. I wish myself and you, dear readers, that with this book we will come one step closer to this goal.

Our deepest fear is not that we are insufficient.

Our deepest fear is to be excessively strong.

It's our light, not our darkness

that scares us the most.

[...]

Keeping yourself small is not serving the world.

There's nothing enlightened about making you small

so that others around you don't feel insecure.

We are all meant to shine like children do.

[...]

It is not just in some of us, but in each and every one of us. And when we let our own light shine, we unconsciously give other people permission to do the same.

When we have freed ourselves of our own fear, our presence automatically frees others.